# Social Measurement

*Points of View of*
*Sociologists*
*Businessmen*
*Political Scientists*
*Government Officials*
*Economists*
*CPAs*

## AI**CPA**
American Institute of Certified Public Accountants

# To the Reader

THIS LITTLE BOOK offers you a chance to eavesdrop on a stimulating conversation.

The participants were a small group of specialists with widely different backgrounds—social and political scientists, business executives, government officials, certified public accountants.

Despite the diversity of their backgrounds, they shared a common interest—an interest in the development of more useful and reliable methods of measuring the effectiveness of social programs.

The search for new measurement techniques has become increasingly urgent. On a worldwide scale, we have become aware of the fact that a number of perilous races are being run—for example, between a growing population and a limited food supply. In their brilliant book, *Only One Earth*, Barbara Ward and René Dubos have declared: "The two worlds of man—the biosphere of his inheritance, the technosphere of his creation—are out of balance, indeed potentially in deep conflict. And man is in the middle. This is the hinge of history at which we stand, the door of the future opening onto a crisis more sudden, more global, more inescapable, and more bewildering than any ever encountered by the human species and one which will take decisive shape within the life span of children who are already born."

In our own country, we have been engaged for some time in a reappraisal of national objectives—a reappraisal which will result in valid conclusions only if we are armed with adequate data to assess our options. This does not mean that the mere acquisition of such data will clearly reveal the proper course to follow. Choices will still need to be made through our democratic processes. But they can then be made with some understanding of their consequences both in terms of anticipated costs and expected benefits. The task of devising these standards of measurement is not an easy one. It ought to be approached with humility, for we hopefully have learned that the dilemmas confronting this nation are immensely complex—that efforts to solve old problems can often create new ones—that good intentions offer no insurance against bad results.

Above all, it should be obvious that no one can claim a monopoly of wisdom on how best to establish sound benchmarks to gauge our progress—or lack of it—in improving the quality of life. A collective endeavor is required. The skills of various disciplines must be involved in attempts to formulate an effective strategy for organizing social change.

That is why this roundtable was held.

Sponsored by the American Institute, the participants met in a conference center in Charleston, S.C., on Wednesday afternoon, April 5, 1972. An informal get-acquainted dinner was held that evening. The actual discussions began the following morning, at which time the current state of the art of social measurement was explored from a number of perspectives. In the afternoon, the participants divided into two sections to consider the subject in greater detail, based on the morning presentations. They then reconvened to review what each group had to say. The concluding session took place on the following morning.

The meeting produced no instant solutions—no flashes of intellectual lightning which illuminated all that was dark before the conference began.

Yet this record of the Charleston gathering deserves reflective reading. It is based on a tape-recorded transcript—edited only for brevity and clarity.

In reading it, you will be joining the company of some highly intelligent and responsible citizens engaged in a pioneering effort.

You may also become convinced, as did many of those in attendance, that a compelling need exists to organize further joint projects to advance the concept of social measurement. "We do not have," one of the participants said, "the luxury of time to spare."

The meeting in Charleston was a mere beginning—the beginning of what might become an exciting adventure for a good many people. You may well be one of them.

JOHN LAWLER
*Administrative Vice President*
American Institute of Certified Public Accountants

# Roundtable Participants

WALTER T. ALBERS, JR., Ph.D.: Head, Societal Analysis Activity, General Motors Research Laboratory.

RAYMOND A. BAUER, Ph.D.: Professor of Business Administration, Harvard University. President, American Association for Public Opinion Research.

ALBERT D. BIDERMAN, Ph.D.: Research Associate, Bureau of Social Science Research.

ROBERT F. BORUCH, Ph.D.: Assistant Professor of Psychology, Northwestern University. Staff member, Social Science Research Council's project on social experimentation.

RALPH M. BROOKS, Ph.D.: Postdoctoral Research Associate, Department of Sociology, Iowa State University.

R. LEE BRUMMET, Ph.D., CPA: Willard J. Graham Professor of Business Administration, University of North Carolina.

BERNARD L. BUTCHER, M.B.A.: Assistant to Executive Vice President, Bank of America, in charge of environmental and social policy.

ANGUS CAMPBELL, Ph.D.: Professor of Psychology and Sociology, University of Michigan. Director, Institute of Social Research.

NEIL C. CHURCHILL, Ph.D., CPA: Royal Little Professor of Business Administration, Harvard University. Director, Management Simulation Exercise, Harvard Business School.

H. JUSTIN DAVIDSON, M.S., CPA: Dean, Graduate School of Business and Public Administration, Cornell University.

ROBERT EISNER, Ph.D.: Professor of Economics, Northwestern University. Member, Research Staff, National Bureau of Economic Research. Member, Executive Committee, American Economic Association.

DAVID C. LINOWES, CPA: Partner, Laventhol Krekstein Horwath & Horwath.

ALICE TEPPER MARLIN: Executive Director and Founder, Council on Economic Priorities.

JAMES B. MCCOMB: Director, Environmental Development, Dayton-Hudson Corporation.

STEWART D. MCELYEA, CPA: Deputy Director, Field Operations Division, U.S. General Accounting Office.

ARTHUR NAFTALIN, Ph.D.: Professor of Public Affairs, University of Minnesota. Mayor of Minneapolis, 1961–69.

WALTER J. OLIPHANT, CPA: President, American Institute of Certified Public Accountants. Senior Partner, Arthur Andersen & Co.

LEONARD M. SAVOIE, CPA: Executive Vice President, American Institute of Certified Public Accountants.

CHARLES L. SCARLOTT, M.S., M.B.A.: Senior Public Affairs Advisor, Standard Oil Company (New Jersey).

PERCY H. TANNENBAUM, Ph.D.: Professor, Graduate School of Public Policy, University of California, Berkeley.

ARTHUR B. TOAN, JR., CPA: Partner, Price Waterhouse & Co. and National Director of Management Advisory Services.

DANIEL B. TUNSTALL, M.I.A.: Staff member, Statistical Policy Division, Office of Management and Budget, Executive Office of the President.

FRANK T. WESTON, M.S., CPA: Partner, Arthur Young & Co.

IAN H. WILSON, M.A.: Consultant, Business Environment Studies, General Electric Company.

———

W. DAVID ANDERSON: American Institute of Certified Public Accountants.

STEWART SCHACKNE: Consultant.

*At the close of dinner on the evening before the seminar,* WALTER J. OLIPHANT, *President of the American Institute of Certified Public Accountants, made the following remarks:*

LADIES AND GENTLEMEN, during the cocktail hour I welcomed some of you informally, and I would now like to say, more formally and to the whole group, that the American Institute is happy to be host at this gathering of distinguished people from a number of disciplines.

When we first began to talk to people in other professions about this roundtable on social measurement, we encountered some reactions of surprise. People wondered why the accounting profession was interested in the subject and what we might be able to contribute to it.

By way of explanation of our interest, let me remind you of a statement by the philosopher Protagoras, "Man is the measure of all things." Certainly, man is the measure of your callings as he is of mine; the several professions which we represent exist to serve human needs. To do this, however, we must know what those needs are.

In times of crisis, men often announce their needs vehemently, sometimes eloquently. For example, the Declaration of Independence holds up the goals of "Life, Liberty and the Pursuit of Happiness." At many times and places people have struggled for "freedom and land." The New Deal proclaimed by Franklin Roosevelt was directed toward that part of the population which was "ill-housed, ill-clad, ill-nourished."

When means are being sought to satisfy basic creature needs such as food and shelter, the degree of success or failure can be measured fairly simply. But in the past few years, a new dimension has come into the discussion of human needs. This new dimension is generally labeled "the quality of life." All of us have a feeling for what that term means, but when we come to trying to improve this "quality," we are often frustrated by its lack of sharp definition.

Today, numerous proposals are made for coping with urban blight, water and air pollution, deficiencies in our educational systems, and many other problems of society. Taken together, the proposed programs would greatly exceed the financial resources available for their realization. How are we to choose among them?

Generally, accountants are regarded by people outside their ranks as concerned mainly with financial information. And to a large extent, that is true. But this idea of the scope of our work is far from complete.

A description of the professional practice of accounting, as enunciated by the American Institute, opens with the statement:

"Accounting is a discipline which provides financial *and other* information essential to the efficient conduct and evaluation of the activities of *any* organization." [Emphasis added.]

In 1967, Joseph M. Goldsen, then with the Rand Corporation, now a Provost at Yale, urged the accounting profession to apply its measurement techniques to the social sector. The following year, at the American Institute's annual meeting, Mancur Olson said that our national income statistics probably are "the finest flower of socioeconomic measurement"—but he added, "Useful as they are, they leave out most of the things that make life worth living, such as the health of the people, the learning of our children, and the condition of our democracy."

Recently accounting firms have been asked to apply their capabilities to such tasks as the measurement of input/output factors in community welfare programs; the cost/benefit ratios of pollution control measures; urban renewal problems, and mass-transit traffic patterns. In studies of these types, the accountants have found themselves working with people from other disciplines, and this experience has led us to believe, first, that in certain areas of social measurement progress will perhaps come faster from interdisciplinary efforts than from the efforts of one profession alone, and, second, that accountancy can make a contribution.

We accountants come to this meeting with specialized expertise but mostly with questions. For example:

In the kinds of social measurement being done now, are there methodologies common to all or some of them?

What are the common interests among people making social measurements at present, and should effort be made to identify these interests in an organized fashion?

Who are the present and prospective users of the products of social measurement, and what are their present and prospective needs?

Apart from the accumulation and classification of data, are the validation and reporting of them adequate?

In the course of our discussions, we will have to take into account not only what data are presently available but what more are needed, with what urgency, and at what cost of accumulation.

We from the American Institute are most pleased that you have agreed to join us in this exploration. I deeply hope it may lead to results that will ultimately serve the public interest.

NEIL C. CHURCHILL, *Professor of Business Administration at Harvard University, opened the Thursday morning session as follows:*

WE HAVE COME to examine a problem as troublesome as it is fascinating. Some of us are concerned with social measurement from a national or macro level and others of us from a micro or single-enterprise level. Some of us are concerned with the normative aspects of the problem, others are trying just to measure their firm's socially related actions. Speaking for the group that organized this roundtable, it is our belief that in the day and a half lying before us we may be able to learn a fair amount from one another. That at least is the intent of the roundtable—to facilitate an exchange of views and experiences, and perhaps to develop some new ways to approach a common problem.

Our format is mostly open and unstructured. The organizing group felt, however, that we could best start off by taking a look at how some disciplines or areas of activity conceive of the problem of social measurement and by having a representative from each of the different areas comment upon what is going on in his field; what information needs are perceived; what difficulties are being encountered, and so on.

Let me underscore that we do not plan to discuss whether business, government, or any other organization *should* be concerned with socially relevant action. We are taking that as an assumption. Therefore, we hope to focus on what should be measured and how the measurements might best be done.

*Churchill introduces* RAYMOND A. BAUER, *Professor of Business Administration, Harvard University.*

PROF. BAUER: I have been asked to talk about how a social scientist approaches the topic of social measurement. If I may take the readings which have been distributed to us as a guide to the interests of this group, I infer that the interests range from evaluation of the performance of a business firm or other institution to evaluation of the performance of society as a whole. The scope is large; therefore, so is the number of perspectives from which a social scientist may approach the problem.

I am a social psychologist and am particularly interested in the measurement of subjective states. With all of us here concerned in one way or another with "the quality of life," the measurement of subjective states is quite central to all our interests. Ultimately the quality of life—fuzzy as that term is—has to be defined in terms of human experience.

I take note that the quality of life is sometimes defined, at least in part, in terms of our physical environment. I am taking the stand that the quality of our physical environment is irrelevant unless it is translated into human experience, and that that human experience is best measured, in almost all instances, in terms of how people feel about it.

You may wonder why I qualify my statement by saying "in almost all instances." Sheer logic compels me to acknowledge that we might be poisoned without noticing it by drinking water with a delicious taste. In that instance, I suppose you might want to question the appropriateness of our subjective state as the measure of the quality of life.

There is another matter on which you might want to challenge the appropriateness of taking measures of subjective states as indicators of the quality of life. This relates to the unconscious—mental illness and associated matters. While there may be few orthodox Freudians among us, I assume that most of us give at least some credence to the notion that a person may be in a state of euphoria but headed for bad times by virtue of his internal dynamics. This matter is not totally amenable to research methods employed by social psychologists, but I will later mention some approximations that have been used, apparently with a certain amount of validity. While the theologian or psychoanalyst may take issue with my premise in some instances, subjective states are a very important matter.

I present to you this morning two propositions. The first is that the quality of life is on the whole best defined in terms of human subjective reaction. The other is that people's subjective reactions can at best be inferred imperfectly from our knowledge of objective circumstances.

The suggestion that the quality of life is best defined in terms of human subjective reaction presumes that we will be able to define human happiness and identify its causes. These having been intractable objectives over mankind's history, I propose that we give empiricism a try. To find out if people are happy, suppose we just ask them. This has, in fact, been done. Studies employing this approach have been reported in two volumes put out by the National Opinion Research Center. One, called *Studies in Happiness*, was published in 1965; the other, *The Structure of Psychological Well-Being*, came out in 1969. In each instance the senior author was Norman Bradburn.

The key question the NORC asked was: "Taken altogether, how would you say things are these days—would you say you are very happy, pretty happy, or not too happy?"

If you were an American in the mid-Sixties, you were likely to report that you were happy under the following circumstances: you were young, well-educated, rich, and white. It did not matter if you were a man or woman.

It was particularly important to be rich. Only 18 percent of people with family incomes under $2,000 said they were very happy, in contrast with about 40 percent of those who had an income of $8,000 and up. (It is hard to say what happened over $8,000 because sample sizes started getting small.)

Whites were about twice as likely to say they were very happy as were blacks, but this was in large part, although not entirely, because they were richer. In every thousand-dollar age-bracket, whites were more likely to say they were happier than were blacks. It seemed to take a little more than a thousand dollars of extra income to bring blacks up to the white level—in part, possibly, because of differences in family size. Education *per se* did not improve the avowed happiness of blacks appreciably, perhaps indicating a rise in level of aspiration that ran ahead of attainment.

Such sensible relationships indicate that this simple straightforward question must be measuring something meaningful. One would not expect the relationships to be perfect, however, and they are not—not all old, poor, undereducated, or black people report they are not happy.

Further evidence of the validity of the answers is the fact that they correlate highly with other subjective measures, such as that one would like to continue his or her life in pretty much the way it is going.

Two other interesting measures that Bradburn used are what he calls a dimension of positive effect and a dimension of negative effect. The dimension of positive effect rests on answers to such questions as whether the person is pleased at having accomplished something, proud of having been complimented, particularly excited or interested in something, and the like. Negative effect is measured by answers to questions about being bored, upset because one has been criticized, being very lonely or depressed.

Both scales correlate strongly with overall reported happiness. But they do not correlate with each other. Positive and negative experiences, while they appear to relate to overall happiness, seem to stem from different sources, and the experience of one does not seem to affect either the experiencing or perception of the other.

Bradburn conducted several waves of interviews in which he re-interviewed the same people, and the answers are quite stable.

Bradburn also made the interesting experiment of testing the impact of the assassination of President Kennedy on his measures. This was done by re-interviewing people whom he had interviewed before the assassination. By and large, the event did not seem to affect the basic sense of well-being except for a considerable increase in the proportion of persons who said they were excited or interested in something and who said they felt depressed and unhappy.

I mentioned earlier the attempts to measure some of the psychological states that are not too close to immediate consciousness. There is, of course, a long tradition of psychiatric and psychological testing to get at such phenomena, but here I am talking about measures which can be used by someone like the average survey interviewer. Batteries of such instruments have been developed generally in connection with field studies of the epidemiology of mental health, or to aid in quick, rough screening for the armed forces. These instruments have been validated against more complex means of psychological and psychiatric assessment. They claim to measure such syndromes as depressiveness, anxiety, grief, and so on.

I do not want to be accused of overstating the usefulness of such measuring instruments, nor would I disguise for a moment that there has been controversy over at least some of the studies with which such techniques are associated. I merely want to note that they exist and that I think they have enough merit to make them worth trying out in some situations.

Two measures Bradburn used in re-interviews after the Kennedy assassination were a grief symptom index and an anxiety symptom index. The grief symptom index employed questions about feeling nervous and tense, having trouble getting to sleep, smoking more than usual, and feeling more tired than usual. The anxiety symptom index bore down on psychosomatic symptoms of nervousness, dizziness, and so on.

The apparent effect of the assassination was to increase scores on the grief symptom index and to leave the scores on the anxiety symptom index essentially unchanged, with a suspicion that it may actually have gone down a little in the white population. If the latter phenomenon seems anomalous to you, Bradburn's earlier study indicated that people's concern with personal problems decreased during the Cuban missile crisis. These findings are consistent with a number of observations that concern over personal problems, and even the incidence of neurosis, goes down in crises.

So much for Bradburn's findings. I might have cited other attempts to get at the quality of life, but this work is distinguished by the use of a variety of measures, and particularly by that one key device of asking people if they were happy.

Although some aspects of his work seem to me unsatisfactory as, for example, his attempts to get at sources of gratification in one's major life roles, such as in marriage, on the job, and so on, I think Bradburn's findings at least indicate that there is solid promise in subjective measures of the quality of life. When one looks at the range of data he gathered and considers what was not reported as well as the ambiguity of some that was, it's clear there is work still to be done. We may hope for further refinements and insights from work in progress at the Institute for Social Research at Michigan.

In opening these remarks I said I would address myself to the idea of the quality of life in terms of subjective states, and, aside from that, to the desirability of having subjective measures of reactions to phenomena concerning which an understanding of how people perceive them is as important as an understanding of "what actually happened." That is, understanding the relationship between objective facts and subjective reaction may be highly informative.

The Bureau of Census is now beginning a series of what are called "victimization surveys" in which a large sample of people are interviewed about any crimes of which they may have been the victim. This type of survey is intended as an alternative to the present system of reporting crime merely by numbers of incidents in various categories.

Certainly the impact of crime on its victims and their response to this experience is an important matter. You can readily think of a string of questions that you would want to ask of a person whose house was entered, whose wallet was stolen from an office, or who was beaten. If crime increases, do people become increasingly apprehensive? Does this apprehension generalize to a loss of faith in society? Is there a reaction against social groups which account for most of the crime? Is this true of part of the population, but not of others?

A very interesting study of the relationship of objective circumstances to subjective perceptions was reported by Peter Rossi in the September 1970 issue of *The Annals*, a publication of the American Academy of Political and Social Science, under the title "Local Political Leadership and Popular Discontent in the Ghetto." Rossi chose to look at two issues: police brutality and unscrupulous business practices in 15 cities, with special concentration on what went on in the ghetto. He interviewed 40 merchants and 50 policemen in each city to get their estimate of the extent of these practices and he then interviewed the residents to get their perception of the incidence of these abuses.

There was an interesting difference between the two issues. Ghetto residents' perception of the incidence of police brutality correlated quite nicely with the "objective" estimate by the police and merchants. There was a smaller correlation between ghetto residents' satisfaction with merchants and the self-reported business practices of these merchants. Rossi also examined whether either of these forms of abuse had been made an issue by local political or community leaders. In both instances the correlation between "reality" and perception increased where the topic had been made an issue by the leadership. However, the correlation increased considerably more for sharp business practices than for police brutality.

What emerges from Rossi's study is the notion that social phenomena of this sort vary in the extent to which perceptions of them are formed via direct experience and observation (e.g., police brutality) and via interpretation by some outside party (sharp business practices). It is an example of how we might better understand the mechanisms whereby objective circumstances are converted into subjective states, something we need to know more about in the social arena.

In the readings which were distributed to us, Angus Campbell makes a plea for collecting data on three subjective indices: "Quality of the Work Experience," "Index of Community Reward," and "Index of Official Insolence." I would advocate both the development of a considerable number of continuing series of subjective measures of these sorts as well as analytical studies such as Rossi's which enable us better to understand the relationship between the objective and the subjective.

I believe that most of these things I have mentioned represent in some meaningful sense measures of the quality of life in various contexts and with varying degrees of specificity. In other instances such measures represent diagnostic aids which can help us to understand how our society works and to improve our social programs.

The point I want to close on is the issue of "hard" versus "soft" data. Let me make a flat assertion: the proposition "Thirty percent of a cross-sectional sample of American adults 18 years and over said they are very happy" is just as objective as the statement that the GNP of the U.S. is one trillion dollars. It may also, in fact, be more accurate. If the operations whereby subjective states are measured are adequately specified, the data are objective in any sense of that word that I know. The problem that bothers one is not the objectivity of the data—a person either said it or he didn't—but the meaning that may be attached to it or the inferences that may be drawn from it.

The problem of the meaning that may be attached to subjective responses and the inferences that may be drawn from them is indeed a knotty one. But, the meaning that may be attached to GNP and the inferences that may be drawn from it are not easy either.

The final answer to the meaning to be attached to subjective responses and the inferences that can be made from them comes out in analysis and use. For example, the fact that someone has a discretionary income of $3,000 does not tell us whether he will spend it on an automobile or on a garage full of Wheaties. But economists have learned that they can nevertheless make certain useful inferences from the data on discretionary income.

My point is that we can develop useful subjective measures only by the empirical process of making such measures and trying them out.

We will make mistakes. But we can also be confident that a fair percentage of the time we will be on target and that we will develop measures whose usefulness will increase as we gain practice with them.

Ms. MARLIN: In questionnaires to elicit subjective perceptions, how do you deal with the difficulty that respondents may not have had experiences that enable them to make comparisons? For instance, a child born in the city doesn't miss trees, grass, or open fields because he hasn't that reference point. He may tell you the city is dirtier or more crime-ridden than it has ever been before, but he has no way of knowing what it is like to have cities in which such conditions do not exist.

Similarly, people asked what they'd be willing to pay for cleaner air may be unaware of the magnitude of the present costs in terms of higher medical bills, cleaning costs, and maintenance costs.

BAUER: This is a difficulty; we have tracked too few questions of that sort over time.

PROF. CAMPBELL: Every time I fly over New York City I look down and think, if all those people down there on the sidewalk could see what they are walking around in, they'd leave. The capacity for adaptation complicates the problem. Pollution insinuates itself gradually; we get used to it; we don't notice the change and pretty soon the condition has reached a point where it's immensely hard to handle.

PROF. TANNENBAUM: A related issue, I think, is how to determine the causes of subjective reports of change. Maybe it isn't so bad to live under certain conditions but suddenly we are told it's bad. How much of today's volatile environment is perhaps the result of suggestion? The factors that lead people to respond the way they do may be the result more of publicity than of actual conditions.

CAMPBELL: Yes, I think there's a lot of half-baked commentary going on these days—what I call popular sociology—about the generation gap and civil disorders and so on without much evidence offered whether this sort of thing is peculiar to our age and, if so, to what degree. Unless we have some base-line, we are really not in much of a position to say whether things have changed or not.

DR. BIDERMAN: More than is usually the case, Ray's presentation has concentrated on the psychological background of the problem of social measurements. His discussion dealt primarily with the subjective measures and he mentioned some qualifications on the applicability of such a basis of measurement. There are many more—the individual's psychic state at the moment of responding, general state of health, vitality, all the aspects of a social system with which he identifies himself. I would like to stress the need for objective and social measurements as well as subjective and individualistic ones.

I think the crime victimization rate study is an example of this. The interesting thing about this survey is first of all that it showed victimization is actually rare—so much so that to do a survey of victimization takes a massive sample to get any representation of the heterogeneous phenomena involved—50,000 cases would be a minimum adequate national sample.

Another reason a large number of people have to be approached to obtain an adequate sample for interview apparently is that the impression made by being a victim of crime isn't retained very long. If you ask people about events of more than six months ago, you have an appreciable loss; and if you ask about anything that happened more than a year ago, you get very little recall of actual events.

Furthermore, if you ask merely a general question about whether they were a victim of a crime last year, you will get some very small fraction of all the victimization. Most crimes do not have major lasting consequences for the victim.

Yet crime obviously is not a trivial thing; it's one of the most important things going on in our social system. Quite aside from people's conception of its importance—that is, its importance to them in having been victimized recently—the threat of crime to the social order, on which so much else depends, is a measurable factor of the quality of life. Here the objective facts seem to be more relevant than individual subjective reactions.

BAUER: The forgetfulness of people who are interviewed certainly is relevant. You see this in the area of consumer research where the importance of the event clearly affects the duration of recall. If you ask people if they bought an automobile in the last year, for example, even if they bought it thirteen months ago, they will probably answer "yes." However, they would under-report the buying of loaves of bread during the year. In asking about loaves of bread, you would have to ask how many loaves of bread did you buy yesterday or in the past week.

PROF. EISNER: Professor Bauer has compared responses to the question of how happy you are with the GNP. I am not an all-out critic of GNP data. I think they are useful and am very much concerned with extending them. Of course, if you want information on subjective responses, you can obtain it. If you find that 30 percent of the sample of respondents say they're happy, that is an accurate figure on what you started out to get—namely, a measure of subjective feelings. But in economics we are particularly interested in behavior, a measure of people's *acts*. The things that concern us generally as regards to quality of life are variables in human behavior. For example, if pollution in a city makes people want to move out of the area and they try to sell their houses and the value of houses goes down, we have a distinct measurement of deterioration of the quality of life.

But we have to be clear about what we are trying to find out. If we're trying to find out how people answer questions about happiness, we can get just as accurate information as we can about GNP. Even though Professor Bauer pointed out that income is a good predictor of how happy people will say they are, if my question were how happy people say they are, I'd rather ask them directly than try to predict how happy they'll be on the basis of income data. But if my question is how people are going to vote, or whether they are going to take part in a demonstration, or something else of that sort, then we might find this to be a matter of both objective and subjective measurement. We cannot have a hard and fast rule on this, and in this connection I would remind you of the considerable amount of work that has been done at the University of Michigan on consumer intentions. Sometimes we can get an idea of what the consumer is going to buy by asking questions about his state of optimism. But if what we are trying to predict and measure is social trends, I do have a preference for looking at current behavior rather than the subjective description of a state of mind which we somehow hope will lead to a prediction of behavior.

BAUER: I think I would agree with you. At the same time, I might be interested in types of people who didn't move out of an area when, if they were in their right minds, it would look as if they should. I would like to find out why. These things depend indeed on what our objectives are, and one of my objectives is understanding as well as prediction.

MR. TOAN: I am surprised that you social scientists aren't much more interested in measuring more directly the effectiveness of the objectives of the various *institutions* of our society, and the effectiveness with which these objectives are being accomplished.

BIDERMAN: You are talking about two different things. One involves monetary values at the level of individuals. This is the fundamental basis of political and economic theory; the ultimate measure is individual satisfaction. Much of the effort of the social sciences, however, goes into attempts to understand the characteristics of systems that make them effective and durable, without attempting to trace to any specific participant or individual his material satisfactions. Because of preoccupation with what amounts to hedonistic assumptions, the measurement apparatus we use neglects to a remarkable degree, in my view, this latter kind of measurement. I think crime statistics, taken from the normative perspective of direct harms to individuals, are not nearly as important to social measurement as taking them as an indicator of the strength and operation of the social system.

BAUER: Crime statistics are certainly not as good as they should be, and you commented that crime from a hedonistic point of view seems unimportant. Now, it's interesting that we wouldn't have known that if we hadn't made these particular measurements. I think we would intuitively have thought that to be robbed would be extraordinarily disturbing. My wife has had her wallet stolen twice during the last year; I've had mine stolen once; and our house was broken into, but we aren't terribly disturbed.

MR. WILSON: We need both kinds of measurement—the accounting type of indicators (that is, a measure of how well are our present policies and programs performing) and the predictive type. I think that we in business are going to be increasingly concerned with some predictive indicators. We have to get feedback on how we've performed, but we also need indicators of how public and private values, aspirations, and goals may be changing and so indicating needed changes in institutional response.

*Chairman Churchill introduces* JAMES B. MCCOMB, *Director, Environmental Development, Dayton-Hudson Corporation.*

MR. MCCOMB: The quality of life is difficult to define and measure because it means different things to different people. Someone moving from an apartment into a home with a large lawn might feel: "This is a great improvement in my quality of life." Someone else might look at the same house and say: "All that lawn to mow—I'd rather live in an apartment."

One of the broad charges given our department is to assist local officials to implement programs to improve the quality of life within the communities in which we have stores—particularly within the central city.

Five years ago, few companies had staffs working on community problems. Each year the number of companies with departments of this nature has expanded as businessmen recognized that they have a responsibility to the communities in which they operate. Business activities in the community must be coordinated with local government and have to be supported by basic community institutions.

As businessmen become more involved in community problems they will desire more information on the results—to determine if there is progress. Some firms are already asking for measurements in these areas. Social responsibility measurements may have to follow an evolutionary process similar to that of the GNP indicators. These indicators are constantly being revised to reflect more accurately the changes that are taking place in our economy. The First National Bank of Minneapolis has begun some work in this area by identifying 10 possible components of a social accounting system for our metropolitan area: Job Opportunities, A Healthy Physical Environment, Good Housing, Good Health, Adequate Income Levels, Quality of Education, A Safe Society, High Level of Citizen Participation, Widespread Cultural Activities, and Adequate Transportation. This is an attempt to measure the overall social health of the community.

Developing measurements that will enable businessmen to examine the impact of their business on the quality of life within the community would be most helpful. Almost all business activities have an impact on the quality of life—either positive or negative. It is virtually impossible to be truly neutral. It could be argued that retailers have played a significant role in improving the quality of life in America by improving the distribution system, so that products could be mass produced at reduced cost and made available to broader segments of society at lower prices. On the other hand, retailers, at times, have been overzealous in the promotion of products. Also, there undoubtedly are items on our shelves that could have a detrimental impact on our quality of life.

The large amount of solid waste created by the retail business is certainly a negative impact on our quality of life. The packaging involved in the distribution system from manufacturer to the ultimate consumer is voluminous. In the past, most of this solid waste was incinerated. In some cases, we were able to recycle paper packaging if a paper plant was located nearby. However, as a result of stricter pollution regulations, we no longer incinerate our refuse. We have installed compacters in our stores and the refuse is hauled away. This solves our problem, but it enlarges the community's problem. Now, more landfill sites will be needed to handle the additional volume of solid waste.

Retailers operate large fleets of delivery trucks that contribute to traffic congestion and pollution. We tested use of propane fuel on several of our vehicles and found, all things considered, that propane was more expensive than gasoline. The reduced maintenance costs did not offset the higher cost of the propane fuel. However, propane does significantly reduce pollution; but we get no credit on our income statement for our contribution to cleaner air. Instead, the use of propane appears as an increased cost.

The two examples cited reflect business decisions of only one company. The overall operation of business and industry affects the quality of life of a community and its citizens. For example, in one community where we have a store, manufacturing plants are spread throughout the area. As a result, they are impossible to serve by public transit. In fact, one plant with 3,000 employees is about five miles from the nearest community. We were shocked to learn that at many companies a prospective employee had to own a car to be considered for employment—in other words, no car, no job.

This city has a large low-income minority population living in the core area. These citizens do not have the income to buy a car and they can't get a job without owning a car. This must be a most frustrating problem for these inner-city residents. Moreover, the city's public bus system is on the verge of bankruptcy and is quite inadequate to fulfill the community's transportation needs.

Crime is a major problem in this area and has reached the point where new housing developments are being surrounded with fences. No doubt the rise in crime has a number of causes. Yet, we can't help but wonder what effect the policy of requiring an automobile to get a job has on the increase in crime.

Social measurements are needed to provide businessmen with information as to the general cost to society of a ton of solid waste, carbon monoxide air pollution, or the benefits of a plant which is located in an area that can be served by convenient public transit. Information of this type could have an important effect on many business decisions. I'm convinced that most businessmen do not consciously set out to increase costs to society; the problems occur because the businessmen do not have adequate information as to the impact of their operations on society.

Rather than relying on government regulations to force business to achieve social objectives, we should concentrate on measuring the costs of certain actions or conditions, and the impact they have on society. Information of this nature can produce socially desirable actions on the part of business. Cost-benefit analysis is used more frequently for programs in the public sector. Several such analyses have been performed for proposed rapid transit systems in this country. Cost-benefit analysis has also been used to measure the benefits of a regional open space program. There are many interesting and innovative ways in which cost-benefit studies could be used to measure the cost to society of privately determined actions.

Yesterday, I visited a department store that has an absolute policy of taking back any merchandise item under any circumstances—no questions asked. This is certainly an excellent service for the consumer, but it is also expensive for the company. They have the highest merchandise return rate in the industry—which is readily believable—but they also quickly point out they have high sales. They don't know, however, to what extent and in what way the return rate relates to the higher sales. If a program like this were to be suggested to our management, they would want to know if an incremental increase in sales would cover the cost of implementing the new return policy. It's my personal belief that a program like this would benefit the company through increased sales. Yet, we don't have a method to determine if this would actually occur.

The manager proposing a program of this nature is at a disadvantage in competing for budget allocations with the manager who projects that a new shopping center or store will produce a return of 12 percent. There is a real need for measurement methods that will demonstrate to management that implementing a program with benefits to society will also provide benefits to the company.

Cost-benefit studies should be used to determine the cost-benefit relationships between programs and policies of the private and public sectors. A program undertaken by business may provide large benefits to society at little cost to the company. Under the present system, the benefits are unmeasured—only the costs to the company are measured.

As we all know, the numbers reported each year as profits are not absolutely precise. To determine profits, a number of assumptions must be made. Application of the same assumptions over a period of years provides a good idea of whether the company is progressing or not. Possibly, the definition of profit should be modified to include social factors that will enable managers to consider additional factors in making everyday business decisions.

DEAN DAVIDSON: Does your company have any solid estimates of the costs of its social programs?

McCOMB: No, we really don't. As yet, we haven't taken a good look at it. We've discussed a social audit, but how do you begin to get at all the significant items? As you know, the Bank of America has worked on this, and they began to run into these fuzzy areas of do-you-count-it-or-don't-you?

MR. BUTCHER: I think he's right that at this stage of the game it makes more sense to look at individual socially-related programs and to consider whether they can reasonably be judged to promise benefit, rather than try to set up an overall social cost budget. Because if, as we have done so far, you come up only with a listing of costs and no way of judging benefits, that is a deterrent to doing more. Management will look at the figures and put them in the same category with the company's annual contribution budget. That's philanthropy and not a way to get management to step out and do more, in a more positive way, in the social field.

MR. LINOWES: In talking of social costs in terms of dollars you are attempting to convert them into our traditional way of measuring things that go on in business. You begin with a premise that the profit-and-loss statement is the place to present these costs, and therefore that social costs should be lumped with the more ordinary costs incurred by a business entity. But perhaps the time has come for us to think about another form of recording and of giving visibility to these other kinds of cost.

Maybe we should begin thinking of adding another dimension to periodic reporting, just as we have added the statement of source and application of funds to the customary profit-and-loss statement and balance sheet. You might have something in the nature of a separate socio-economic operating statement, a statement that would somehow quantify the positive and negative effects on society of actions taken by the business organization during the period being reported.

I can't believe it is ever going to be possible to transform social costs into the traditional forms of business reporting where all costs and gains are expressed in monetary terms.

McCOMB: That is a good suggestion. The problem many of us face in business is translating what is happening in society into terms that fit the frame of reference most familiar to businessmen. Profits, of course, are the salient element of that frame of reference, particularly if the company is publicly held.

EISNER: There is a basic question here that goes beyond measurement and the way that measurement should be done. I think we might well consider the position of the economist Milton Friedman and others who question whether it is up to a corporate enterprise to do good for society outside its normal economic activity and to make decisions as to how society can be improved. The best way to deal with social cost may be by a pattern of tax exemptions and subsidies, which would leave business free to pursue maximization of profits as a goal but under constraints and incentives that would be beneficial to society. To ask businesses voluntarily to do things in the interests of society is inconsistent with profit motivation and raises questions as to whether businesses are qualified to do it. I don't know whether business leaders are any more enlightened than university leaders or anyone else. Are we willing to accept their judgments in this field?

If they are competent in running their own businesses in the interest of making profit, I would be satisfied with that, and I wouldn't want anyone to interfere with this function of theirs. The answer to an inclination, say, to make profits at the cost of intolerably increasing urban congestion is to lay a tax on automobiles and other transportation systems. Businesses that pollute the environment should be deterred by taxes. But otherwise I don't know how you can involve businesses in accounting for something, namely, social costs and benefits, which has nothing to do with their prime purpose. Why should they try to account for losses they impose on society when they are not actually penalized for those losses? It would be preferable, I think, to set up a governmental institutional framework which would see to it, as far as possible, that businesses pay for the costs that they inflict—then they can decide whether it's worthwhile inflicting those costs and paying the tax, or finding some other method of producing.

BAUER: My concern is that there will always be issues coming along on which a consensus has not developed to the point where government itself can clarify what should be done.

EISNER: Yes. The South African example is a good one. I hardly think we should look to business enterprise to set national policy in that regard. I have some strong feelings about the white leaders of South Africa, but I think that those who are trying to exert pressure for change there by telling businesses to scrap their investments in South Africa are on the wrong track. To expect that kind of write-off of investment is absurd. If we are going to take action in this regard, the place to do it is at the ballot box.

DAVIDSON: I want to come back to the question of whether measuring social actions by business should be part of the normal measurement and reporting of profit or loss. I suggest that present financial statements don't do an adequate job of distinguishing short-term and long-term profit. Existing profit-and-loss statements reflect the effects of what previous managements of the company have done in prior years and what the present management has done in the current year. We don't get a good reading on what the management of a company has accomplished this year with respect to long-term profitability.

CAMPBELL: I would like to go back to something Mr. McComb said, and ask whether he really intended to say what he did and, if so, how his company feels about it. I'm speaking of cost-benefit analysis; you referred specifically to the *costs* to the *company* and the *benefits* to *society*. You mean that?

McComb: Yes.

Campbell: . . . the costs to the company without any regard for the benefits to the company but only benefits to society? Is that right?

McComb: This is the problem. We'll have to work on a method to measure this.

Campbell: No, it isn't a matter of measuring. . .

Linowes: I think there is another element here we should not lose sight of and that is that what most businesses do is in fact good for society. A company that produces milk, a company that produces clothing, incurs costs for profit-making purposes, but as long as the operation is good for society we should certainly recognize it as highly desirable and commendable.

Marlin: But how do we make those decisions? Are electric carving knives good for society? Are atomic bombs? Tranquilizers? In more economic terms, how does their benefit to society compare with their cost in terms of pollution, exhaustion of natural resources, and, most telling of all, in terms of their opportunity cost? In other words, what could those same human, natural and time resources buy? Better health care? Adequate food, clothing and housing for more people? Pollution control equipment? Education in science or in human relations? And though businesses produce "goods," they also produce "bads," both externalities like pollution and harmful products, such as thalidomide or an unsafe car.

*Chairman Churchill introduces* DANIEL B. TUNSTALL *of the Statistical Policy Division, Office of Management and Budget.*

MR. TUNSTALL: Let me begin with a description of what I do in government. I work in the Statistical Policy Division of the Office of Management and Budget, descended as of July 1970 from the Bureau of the Budget. The Office of Management and Budget is part of the overall Executive Office of the President. Although I will talk primarily about work going on in the federal government, today I am a private citizen and my views are only my own.

The main focus of our work in the last two-and-a-half years has been to develop a publication of national social indicators.

Most of you, I know, are familiar with the book, *Toward a Social Report*, published in 1969 by the Department of HEW. It was intended to do at least four things—identify important social information which may be called social indicators; analyze social conditions to determine whether things are getting better or worse; interpret the major causes of conditions; and, last, indicate what the government reaction should be to social problems.

Although people in both the Johnson and Nixon administrations tended to disregard the thinking that led to *Toward a Social Report*, there was a great deal of interest in it elsewhere. It has sold more than 60,000 copies, and sales continue. However, a number of people judged that it tried to do too much, and the decision was made to split statistical development from social analysis. It was believed that the federal government could develop social indicators, leaving the more difficult tasks of analysis and interpretation to private research groups and universities. The work on statistics was assigned to the Bureau of the Budget in July 1969—to what was at that time the Office of Statistical Standards, now the Statistical Policy Division.

I should note some of the earlier history of social reporting. Several early publications influenced the HEW work. For example, the report of President Eisenhower's Commission on National Goals in 1960 spelled out in considerable detail a range of national goals which commission members believed could be attained in this, the decade of the 1960s. Going still further back, the predominant U.S. effort in social reporting research was directed by William Fielding Ogburn under President Hoover. The published volume called *Recent Social Trends* consisted of a basic social report of 75 pages and a series of monographs analyzing social change in 30 different areas. I think it is important to realize that the summary report of the Research Committee on Social Trends included sections dealing with the problems of our physical, biological, and social heritage. To some extent we still rely on the work of the sociologists and economists who participated in that research.

More personally, my thinking was influenced by Nestor Terleckyj while working at the National Planning Association on a project to develop a methodology to analyze the achievement of national goals.

As we began to develop a set of social indicators, the main question faced, assuming we would not interpret social change nor propose policy changes, was how to determine what statistics to collect. There was already a *Statistical Abstract*—a very good one—with about 1,000 pages of various types of data, updated each year. There were also a United Nations *Compendium of Social Statistics* and a number of other publications similar in content. So why do this again? That was not our purpose.

Instead, with a rough model of national social goals based on our own best judgment, we then broke down these large goal areas into constituent parts which could be measured with existing statistical series.

By September 1970 we submitted three draft chapters (income, education, and employment) along with a general outline to an evaluation committee made up of experts outside the government and to an Interagency Committee made up of the heads of major federal statistical agencies. We also sent these materials to the Domestic Council for their consideration. By the beginning of 1971 it was fairly clear that these three groups agreed we were developing a useful product. Personally, I feel that we may not have done some things very well at that point, but we hadn't made any big mistakes either, and the general idea was to keep moving. We spent most of '71 working on four more chapters.

Within a couple of weeks we will send to our ad hoc committee six draft chapters and a general introduction for their review and comment. Our intention is to issue a publication called *Social Indicators* in early 1973. Many people in this audience have heard me talk about this project before, and each time the target date gets later and later. Those of you who are familiar with the literature and debate surrounding this work know there has been some opinion that this is something that can be done very quickly. In fact, we had thought we would be able to do the job relatively quickly by putting out a publication of social indicators that would be rather like publications of economic indicators. It has taken quite a bit of time to learn that economic indicators are not entirely applicable as a model. But I think we are moving along.

Let me outline a few of the criteria we used to select information. First of all, I should say the publication will contain charts and tables—a visual communication. Charts involve problems of scale, of time of year, and so on, but we are doing our best to design them so that data are presented in a simple manner. Each chapter includes, along with charts and supporting tables, source notes, definitions, and some exposition on the problems of data collection. There will be introductory text for each chapter and for each set of charts. In some cases, when data are particularly difficult to interpret or believed to be extremely misleading, we have taken the opportunity to describe problems with measurement and have included suggestions for gathering new information.

Now let me give you a glimpse of the major social areas we include. I previously mentioned education, employment, and income. We are also including chapters on health, housing and the physical environment, leisure and recreation, population and family structure, and public safety and legal justice. Within each area we have identified "social concerns."

Let me give you an example of a "social concern." In the area of health, we note two major social concerns (sometimes there may be as many as five, but in health we've found two most useful). The first one is long life; most people want to have long lives, and this desire seems to have a strong influence on social policies. The other one is physical and mental well-being of the population. This covers the range of concern from disability to more positive health.

When identifying social concerns, we try to keep a national point of view. Another aim is to identify concerns that can be related to national policy. Finally, we try to encompass all major national social concerns that can be measured; that is, we attempt to be comprehensive. The reason for this last point is that every major agency of the federal government has done work in these areas in one way or another. HEW publishes data on education, on social security, on health. The Labor Department carries out research and collects data in the area of employment opportunities. Our publication will include statistics needed to measure these and many more concerns.

The selection of indicators to measure these concerns is based on two criteria: we try to select information about individuals and their social well-being, and we try to include a measure of social "outputs" or what may be called the end product of social processes.

By and large, all the indicators are given as national totals and then disaggregated to show age, sex, and race differences. Other breakdowns—income, education, occupation, geographic location of the family or individual—are also included. National totals are also broken down to show components—thus, in health, measures of life expectancy are quite useful indicators of attainment of long life, but it is necessary to show mortality rates in order to understand causes of death. At this point we are forced to use existing data, which are not always adequate to judge social change.

I should point out here that our office is concerned with the development of federal statistics; thus a publication of national social indicators can be useful to review the need for new data, and this review should become part of the planning function of the office. Thus the most important function of publishing social indicators may be to stimulate the development of new kinds of statistics—particularly those needed for planning.

Let me stop here by just noting that our project to develop social indicators has led us to become involved in social indicator and social reporting research in universities and private research organizations, state and local governments, the National Science Foundation, the Organization for Economic Cooperation and Development in Paris, and the U.N. statistical office.

BUTCHER: Is there any effort to weight the several areas you've studied?

TUNSTALL: We made a decision early on not to attempt any sort of weighting nor to try to find links between social concerns. I have seen papers in which the author attempts to combine measures in each area to come up with a grand total for society as a whole. Michael Spartz has taken the *Statistical Abstract*, picked six social areas and combined them into an index, weighting them equally. He has done this for each year of the 1960s to see if any progress can be seen. We are not going to do that with our set of indicators.

BUTCHER: I have his paper here and the best part of it seems to be the listing of its extensive limitations.

TUNSTALL: Yes, there are a great many problems.

PROF. NAFTALIN: What do you take to be the status of legislation on social accounting?

TUNSTALL: I see Herb Jaspers had planned to be here, and if he were, it would be better for him to talk about that. For the last three years both Democratic and Republican spokesmen have testified against the Mondale bill, the Council of Social Advisers, and the writing of a social report. The third part of the most recent testimony, the part on which we are working, is social indicators, and this administration has given support to development of social indicators. Last summer, in testimony we gave on Mondale's bill, we were able to bring out the positive role that social indicators can play.

NAFTALIN: What is the reasoning behind the administration's opposition to the Mondale bill?

TUNSTALL: I brought along copies of the testimony of last summer and I'll let you read it. One argument: there is no need for a Council of Social Advisers because there is a Domestic Council with a large staff and it can do this kind of work for the President. Also, if the President's reorganization plan goes through, each of four major agencies will have an assistant secretary for planning, research, evaluation, and they will be able to get together as their own council and, being more politically oriented, would be more useful to the President.

On the other side, those in favor of the Mondale proposal say, "sure you have a Domestic Council but it is not accountable to the Congress." Instead, representatives of the administration from the various departments come to Congress and say "these are the policies of the administration"—in areas of health, education, welfare, and so on. The administration's bills come to Congress one by one and are considered separately. Mondale's idea is that the interrelationship among social policies and programs should be considered—there should be an overview of society, particularly when we are talking about the future.

TOAN: One would think that for these statistics to be useful in the long run you would have to find some way to relate them to programs or efforts. Right now there is a gap. Over here there is a certain set of numbers and someone has to estimate how they reflect particular conditions and how they might affect ideas for change. Is there, as yet, any sort of organized approach—any thought as to how the data can be brought together with planning?

TUNSTALL: At present there is the Federal Budget, and it is probably the closest thing we have to an overview of major social policy. Otherwise, concerted planning at the national level is not done. In terms of going further in evaluating social programs, many of you have had more experience with that than I have.

DAVIDSON: Are you concerned about the validation problem? Many government figures that are put out are later revised, sometimes substantially. Many of the figures that are published seem open to question.

TUNSTALL: Yes. We worry about that but I don't know what can be done about it. It is as much a problem of specifying objectives as it is a problem of verifying that a particular series measures the objective. That is true in the employment field and even more so in education. Can we say that a test measures pupil achievement or ability?

BAUER: I wasn't quite sure of the sense of Art Toan's question, but very often it's assumed that social indicators can be used for program evaluation. In fact, very early in the social indicator movement, I wrote something like that and got my wrist slapped by Eleanor Sheldon and Howard Freeman who were right that the performance of any one statistical series is likely to be multi-determined and the impact of any one program on the series is certainly partial.

LINOWES: What would happen if the Mondale bill were passed?

CAMPBELL: It would force implementation of everything we're talking about. But I must say I have some real reservations about the bill. Even with the Council of Economic Advisers, who have a tremendous reservoir of data to draw on—far more consequential than the other social scientists have, it is disquieting to see them bent to political interests. As for the rest of us, who don't have the wealth of data to support the advice we might be asked to give, I think we would find ourselves in a very difficult situation, that social science would find itself in a very disquieting situation. I think that if we had a Council of Social Advisers at this minute they would be issuing statements that busing of schoolchildren is not desirable, because that is Mr. Nixon's view. Actually, the arguments on busing are not very convincing one way or another. And if the Coleman report is relevant, then we would be compelled, as representatives of social science, to take positions we probably shouldn't have taken.

TUNSTALL: That's a problem and I have thought about it a great deal. One thing that hinders the creation of a Council of Social Advisers is that there has been so little preparatory work done. I have never read a paper by a social scientist who has discussed in detail what the council should do and what it should not do, or how it would operate, or how the council would work with the Office of Management and Budget where there are already 600 professionals thinking about similar problems, or the relationship of the council with the Domestic Council with over 60 professionals and one or two people who are politically very powerful. I would like to urge social scientists who are interested in this proposal to write about the political role this new council would play instead of merely offering their general support.

DAVIDSON: Let me ask you about use of the data. You haven't talked about that at all. It seems to me that what you've done so far is the easiest part of the task.

TUNSTALL: Yes, I would hope that with publication of the document on social indicators, which will be a fairly substantial achievement if it all goes through, opportunities for application would be apparent to many people. Granted, some people take the attitude that with all these charts and tables we still don't know where we are going. But the answer to your question may not lie at our feet.

We need help from people like yourselves. Help us encourage the Social Science Research Council to develop an Institute for Work on Social Indicators and play an active role in developing better social information. Encourage private groups to do their own social reports.

CAMPBELL: What kind of input does your office get from business, labor, nonprofit organizations, and so on, and how useful is it?

TUNSTALL: Others in the office could answer that question in more detail than I. But I can say it's my observation that business is better organized to make an impact on data collection than are nonprofit social-oriented organizations such as educational and health groups. The business community has, as you know, a Business Advisory Council for Federal Reports that advises the government on the collection of data that affect their interests. It's important, of course, for government to get the views of businessmen to see what can be collected and what is a burden. There is no combined effort on the part of social interests. In that field, the information we get comes as a result of ad hoc arrangements—usually made through federal agencies.

BAUER: I believe that one of the conditions set by Dr. Sheldon on taking her new job was that there would be an office in Washington concerned with social indicators. So it may be that we'll see such an office set up shortly.

*Chairman Churchill introduces* ARTHUR NAFTALIN, *Professor of Public Affairs, University of Minnesota, and former Mayor of Minneapolis.*

NAFTALIN: I have some observations with regard to measurement and social indicators that may appear to be somewhat negative and skeptical, but my intention is to be analytical and not critical. So I hope you will suspend judgment until I am through and we have had some opportunity to discuss the points I am about to make.

You can't be in public life these days without coming to appreciate the value of hard facts, of knowledge, and of accurate measurement of data. There is a direct relationship, I believe, between the command of information and effective political action. In my experience I have often observed leaders achieve objectives in the face of strong opposition because they were able to gather and present information and facts that were persuasive and compelling.

In fact, my interest in this roundtable centers about the relationship between social measurement and how social and political change can be effected. My concern is *not* essentially over the question of the social responsibility of business. As a matter of fact, I feel that businesses operate under such severe limitations—so far as affecting public policy is concerned—that no matter how energetic many of them may be in pursuing social programs they are not likely to do more than nibble at the margins of our major problems. Needed social change depends instead, I believe, on what government does about these problems.

I would like to identify what I think are problems in the matter of social measurement as it relates to governance, referring first to voting behavior, by which I mean public attitudes concerning public policy. It is, of course, an area that has received increasing attention during the last 20 or more years as interest in measuring public opinion has increased in the face of growing social complexity. In terms of its effect on governance, this growing preoccupation with opinion measurement presents a danger that is not fully sensed. We often assume that because we have polls of public opinion we have clear and valid measurement of what the public believes and what it will support in the way of public policy. Thus the polls lead us often to lose sight of the fact that the ultimate policy position of the electorate is the function of a dialectical relationship between followers and leaders and that the poll measures opinion only at a moment in history and does not—perhaps cannot—measure potentially different responses to alternative leadership appeals.

I am thinking, for example, of the book by Richard Scammon and Ben Wattenberg, *The Real Majority*. This book identifies a hard center of political opinion which the authors believe sets the parameters within which feasible political action can occur. Scammon and Wattenberg believe that poll data provide a road map which marks out for the political leader what he must do in order to win public support. I would hold that there are so many uncertainties with respect to what the public believes and what the public can be brought to believe that polling is not an accurate indicator of the potential for eliciting public support for particular positions.

The voter reacts at two levels. At the manifest level—the level of what he articulates as his beliefs—his opinions can be measured with some degree of accuracy. At the latent level there is a substratum of feelings, emotions, and intuitions that are not amenable to articulation and are, therefore, not amenable to valid measurement. But the latent level is often more important than the manifest level insofar as ultimate political action is concerned.

Regard for a moment the contest for the Democratic presidential nomination. Senator McGovern began with 2 or 3 percent in the polls, and the pundits wrote him off. Yet things were happening at a latent level, and they were not being measured. Formless feelings concerning the general social situation were being reflected in the primary votes for McGovern. He was reacting to something latent in the public attitudes, and his reaction was helping this latent feeling to become manifest. In time his standings in the polls began to rise, and this rise altered the parameters of what is perceived to be the limits of possible political action.

When I was Mayor, I viewed this dynamic relationship at close range. It was a time of growing turbulence, and we faced a critical confrontation between those who, on the one hand, were urging a more aggressive policy of social reform in order to ameliorate social conditions and those, on the other hand, who favored a policy of law enforcement that affirmed without qualification the need to maintain law and order. What was interesting to me was the degree to which many individuals and the public generally were ambivalent as regards the two opposing approaches. At one moment a citizen would come down hard on the side of law and order and the next moment the same individual would be on the side of social reform. Polling reflected what was manifest at the moment and it failed to measure what was latent, thus obscuring the public's essential ambivalence. As a result, political leaders were led, in my view, into an all too simple acceptance of what they took to be the manifest demand for aggressively administered law and order.

A second aspect of the relationship between measurement and governance is the matter of aggregating power. How does a democratic society mobilize its publics? How does it organize political momentum so that policies of change will have support? What strategies and techniques will make possible the aggregating of power so that governance can proceed? What accounts for the power of a Billy Graham? What can we learn from this relationship between a leader and his followers that can help us understand how to mobilize support for programs of social change? How can we successfully govern against the grain of public resistance to changes that are essential to our survival?

Most of us would probably agree that there ought to be in operation public policies of a kind that are not likely to have strong support.

We need to know how power can be aggregated in a democratic society to accomplish ends which, on the surface at least, appear to be politically unpopular. We need to know a great deal more than we do about political parties and political movements, and this is clearly an area that requires greatly improved techniques of measurement. It requires social indicators that give us clues to the mysteries of successful political action.

A third dimension in the relationship between measurement and governance is the matter of determining the degree and quality of need. When we talk about social indicators we are really talking about identifying and measuring deficiencies, dysfunctions, dislocations, needs, problems—about getting the hard facts. But the concept of the indicator hides a great value question, because indicators and measurements always state a relationship. When we talk about the degree of poverty or the extent of income or the deficiency in education or health service, we are using indicators that measure social need in relation to a standard, and the standard inevitably involves a value preference. Value preferences are political questions, and measurements, indices, indicators cannot decide for us our value choices. It is important not to be confused on this point. Social indicators can identify deficiencies, dislocations, dysfunctions, but always with respect to assumed norms, and they will not tell us what the "proper" norms are. We arrive at norms as individuals in terms of our value preferences and, as a society, in terms of what we can attain through the political process.

The next consideration is, how do we choose among alternative approaches to ameliorating social problems? This involves us in the measurement of costs and benefits. What are the trade-offs? What does the analysis of policy tell us about the relative merits of particular proposals? What we seek with respect to this dimension is some form of objective measurement that informs us about how close we are coming to realizing our norms, however unclearly they may be defined. This is the world of PPBS, of planning the "best" use of available resources. It is a search for some form of social calculus, the presumption being that an objective measurement of costs and benefits will identify the most productive use of resources and thereby provide a rational and unbiased means of choosing among different value-choices. Clearly this is an area that demands extensive improvement and refinement in measurement techniques before we can accept indicators as providing valid guides.

Next is the matter of the implementation of policy. When public policies are being formulated, the interest and attention of scientists and politicians run strong. Making policy and building new programs are the glamorous part of government, and they command the public's attention. But then comes the stage of implementation and follow-through, and public attention drops as policy execution becomes the responsibility of the nonpolitical bureaucracy. We are discovering now, after many years of effort in antipoverty and other social areas, how little attention we have paid to policy implementation. We are amazed to find that government programs affecting millions have had little or no evaluation, and suddenly we are aware of the need for indicators that will tell us when programs are working and that will measure their value and effectiveness. Once a bill is passed into law, the Congressman or Senator rushes on to a new problem. It's the new proposal that gets the headlines and commands public attention. There is amazingly little testing of programs, very little genuine demonstration effort. Here is an area in which there are much opportunity and need for developing measurement devices that will evaluate and assess the effectiveness of public programs.

I proceed now to my most important point. I will be somewhat autobiographical since it involves the tension that I have found in my work between my academic involvements and my public involvements. Among my political associates I often hear expressions of this type: "You academic people don't really understand the nature of politics. You are doctrinaire, visionary, and unrealistic. You don't know how to work with the public. You are not concerned with their feelings and attitudes, and, as a result, you don't know how to win elections. Your leadership is not respected by the public because you decide your policies without regard to what the public feels is needed." Meantime among my academic colleagues I hear another type of expression, stated with about the same degree of petulance: "You politicians in City Hall! You don't read books. You don't use the findings of social scientists. You don't understand the complexities of a complicated society. You are all the time acceding to the wishes of your constituents without regard to the long-range consequences of yielding to their immediate wants. You follow your constituents rather than lead them."

These are obviously two quite different approaches to the formulation of public policy. If we push the two positions to their extremes, we find—at the academic end—a form of social engineering. The academic view has faith in research, knowledge, and planning; it seeks to build the better society by utilizing science, by deriving from hard facts the standards we should seek to realize. We are all to some extent caught up in this approach. It is the belief that superior intelligence will direct us to superior social action, that what we need is to rise to the level that science makes possible and govern ourselves accordingly. During the time of the New Deal, Rexford Tugwell had recommended the establishment of a directive branch of government, the idea being to give over policy-making to a group which was equipped for the proper exercise of authority. Perhaps, pushed to its ultimate implication, this is what a Council of Social Advisers might be. The idea is, of course, an authoritarian concept—that the scientist, the technocrat, the social planner knows what's best for society, that he has deduced the truth that we should live by from the facts at his command. This is both a philosophical and psychological position based in empiricism: we weigh, count, measure, all of which is nonpolitical and which will tell us what is right and wrong in social policy.

Now at the other extreme—shall we say the political or nonscientific extreme—we find policy-making conditioned by the intuition and hunches of the leader and by the presumed preferences of the constituents. What the people want they shall have, and the political leader measures his success in terms of how he senses and how he meets that demand. Ultimately the mass man rules, his feelings and wants determine policy.

So at one extreme policies are shaped for the people in terms not of what they want but rather of what—in the minds of élitist policy-makers—they *should* want, and at the other extreme policies are shaped not with respect to what intellectual analysis informs us concerning ultimate social consequences but rather by what the people want. The latter emphasis is the seedbed of populism; it is an approach that recognizes as the preferred norm for social action the mass man's view of the good life, and it rejects, in the language of George Wallace, the leadership of the "pointy-headed intellectuals."

The populist view romanticizes the past, because in an earlier stage life was simpler and required less planning and ordering. It thus tends to be reactionary, seeking to restore what is thought to have once existed. The "scientific" view is, on the other hand, forward-looking, holding out the vision that informed planning can produce a new and better social order that will be consistent with the hard facts and the social realities of the times.

This is all prefatory to my major point, which is that, in the relationship between social measurement and governance, knowledge and hard facts must be joined to the public's value preferences, and it is the form and nature of that joining that constitute the central problem of government. This is to argue that—as we evolve a set of social indicators and as we evolve sophisticated methods of measurement—we must not lose sight of the fact that, ultimately, the most important decisions will not be made by scientists or accountants or engineers. They will be made by people in a political context.

Leadership in a democratic society needs social indicators and the capacity to use solid knowledge. But leadership must use facts and knowledge and must never become captive to those instruments.

These, then, are some of my views concerning the relationship between social measurement and governance—views that, given the uncertain state of society and our knowledge concerning it, are unfortunately—but perhaps necessarily—defined very imprecisely and are offered in a most tentative spirit.

CHURCHILL: I trust there are no questions. [*Laughter*]

BIDERMAN: I think Prof. Naftalin's description omits something and that is that there's a kind of élite of the middle, too. In the United States, the people who could be called leaders number in the thousands. No matter how refined your definition of "leader," it's a very large number. There is a large number of élites and large numbers of people in all of them. The people George Wallace talks to, for example, have perceptions about trends in taxation that derive from somewhere other than their own perception. Furthermore, because of rising education, people are increasingly amenable to more accurate perceptions of reality. People have perceptions about the crime situation that I don't see could be derived other than from statistics—the FBI statistics, for instance. I am sure that statistics have played a major role in the development of the perception of these people. I don't think that the relation of measurement to the body politic should be cast exclusively in the framework of the consumer being an official in some agency who uses social readings to make a decision that is implemented by edicts of government. I think that efforts toward a simple presentation of statistics presume that there is a fairly large and fairly lay kind of audience for this kind of information.

DAVIDSON: I gather that Professor Naftalin advocates separating the political process and the measuring process. I don't see how this can be done. Every time one reports a measurement process there is a halo effect. Whatever one chooses to report will affect people's behavior. Take crime statistics. If you report simply the incidence of crime by blacks, that leaves people with one perception. If you report also the percentage of those crimes that are committed *against* blacks, that leaves people with another perception. You can't avoid this halo effect. As long as you're measuring you're going to have that problem.

EISNER: Dr. Naftalin speaks of the need for the political leader to have facts and then translate them into policies people will accept. I think we have a way of overlooking facts that are unpleasant. I'm a great believer in integration, and here the facts are that in many instances integration has been quite costly to large masses of white people—to white children. The fact that the Coleman report cast doubts on a number of aspects of some of the things we might want to do is something that we can't easily shove under the rug. It may be best to try to improve our indicators to bring some of these facts out into the open and to hope we can have political leaders who have the perception and the vision to be attuned to things that I'm afraid the pointy-headed intellectuals have known but the rednecks appreciate very sharply. People are not unaware when they're being pushed around, they know they're suffering—and when enlightened leaders with the information don't react, someone else is going to win the ballgame.

NAFTALIN: Concerning Al Biderman's comment, I don't think I have stated here an élitist concept of leadership. I have stated a concept of leadership that does involve discovering ways of leading against the grain of resistance because in a confused, changing society this is a requirement of leadership. But my point is to do this with fidelity to the democratic process and to delegate to the constituency participation and involvement.

CHURCHILL: Alice, would you tell us how the Council on Economic Priorities operates?

MARLIN: In choosing appropriate means of comparing companies' performances in areas that affect society and are commonly regarded as "externalities" by economists, the Council must choose some measuring stick. We strive to find one that can be applied equally well to each company in an industry. In evaluating pollution control records, for example, we have not chosen compliance with the law as the metric because laws vary widely among states, and enforcement varies even more widely. A plant located in Oregon and constantly in hot water with the state regulatory agency for non-compliance with that state's strict air pollution laws may in fact have far more effective control equipment installed than does a similar plant in Louisiana where the environmental authorities have never moved against the plant and even in informal discussion may regard the plant as quite satisfactory.

Because, at the time of promulgation, it was a state-of-the-art standard and did specify emissions, we could use certain Oregon regulations as a criterion, to see whether mills throughout the U.S. could meet Oregon standards. Both CEP and Arthur D. Little used Oregon's air pollution control regulations for the pulp industry as the standard-to-meet for all similar plants in the U.S.

In general, however, the Council has dealt with this problem by measuring every plant's equipment against the best pollution control equipment commercially available at reasonable cost, a metric that applies equally to all plants, regardless of location. The choice of this state-of-the-art standard does not mean that we advocate the installation of all this equipment at all plants at any cost, just that it is the most universally applicable measuring-stick. To establish some "appropriate" amount of equipment, for example, to establish different standards for urban and rural plants, would require far more extensive use of value judgments, and an unwieldly degree of variation—what about suburban areas, or plants located next door to orphanages or public flower gardens?

In areas where it is more difficult to establish any measure, the most appropriate approach may be to use averages as norms, like the average percentage of employees at each professional level who are minority group members or women, compared with their representation in the population or to the percentage of other racial or sexual group members at that professional level.

*Chairman Churchill introduces* ARTHUR B. TOAN, JR., *Partner, Price Waterhouse & Co. and National Director of Management Advisory Services.*

TOAN: I have been asked to conclude this morning's session by making some comments on the interest of the accountant in social performance measurement. In the process of doing this, I will take some time to tell you something of the work of the accounting discipline in total as well as its interest in the specific topic of this meeting.

The interest of accountants in measurements and the process of measurement is long-standing. In fact, because of the critical importance of *financial* measurement, more money has probably been spent on accounting measurements over a longer period of time than on measurement of any other type. If one were to add to the ranks of accountants in public practice the much larger number of accounting practitioners employed by business, government, and nonprofit organizations, plus the still more numerous individuals whom we call "clerks," and the time of those "very dumb but very smart" machines we call computers, one would surely find in accountancy the greatest mass of measurers ever assembled. Not all their activities have measurement as the primary objective, but a surprisingly large portion do contribute directly or indirectly to the process.

The accountant's interest in social performance measurement evolves quite logically from the knowledge and experience he has accumulated over centuries of producing relevant financial information in an organizational setting for a variety of uses and users. At one time, I suppose, it was possible to interpret the words "accounting" or "financial information" as the equivalent of "monetarized information," for it was, in fact, all financial in the narrow sense of the word.

I can't imagine, however, that this situation lasted very long. As soon as it became apparent that financial data would be more understandable and more useful when coupled with nonfinancial information, the accountant was asked to obtain that information also and to integrate it into financial reports. The accountant, thus, began to serve as the accumulator, summarizer, reporter, and analyst of both financial and nonfinancial data. The trend toward blending both kinds of data continues; in fact, it continues at an accelerated pace.

Just as he was asked to expand the scope of the information produced, so was the accountant or financial executive asked to expand or alter the scope of his activities. From being solely a recorder of history, the accountant was pulled into the center of management as a part of the process commonly known as financial planning and control. Budgets, long-range plans, capital expenditure evaluations, R & D projects, new product planning, and many other financial and semifinancial techniques in which the accounting discipline is involved became important instruments of management. They have come to influence strongly the management of all significant endeavors, most particularly by their impact on the planning and decision-making process, on resource allocation, on directing, measuring, reporting, and communications. They supply, in short, not just a portion of the basis for managing most major organizations but the only existent formal, integrated planning and control mechanism in general use.

All this has intensified the accountant's interest in nonfinancial data. It has, for example, heightened the need to develop methods for compiling financial and nonfinancial information on a comparable basis or for presenting it in an integrated manner. It has brought a need to develop reasonable means for making future projections as well as for recording historical occurrences. It has led the accountant to concern himself with longer time-spans and more complex relationships. It has substantially altered both the scope of accounting as a discipline and its place in an organization.

This is "modern" accounting. Or, perhaps, one should say this is the modern *model* of accounting, for there are many imperfections that exist in our use of accounting as an instrument of planning, as an instrument of recording, and as an instrument of reporting to meet the internal needs of management and the external needs of the public at large.

Accountants and users of accounting data are acutely aware of these problems. You may find some of the problems interesting to you as users and producers of your kinds of information, for they will not be unfamiliar. They include:

the trade-off which must be made between the cost of gathering, summarizing, and analyzing information and its value to those who can use it

the difficulty of designing and operating systems which will produce information on a *timely* basis without the undue sacrifice of accuracy

the problems inherent in the establishment of mutually-agreed-upon definitions and principles as to what is to be gathered and reported the difficulties in communicating accounting results to individuals and groups lacking familiarity with accounting terminology and sophistication in accounting technique

the difficulties involved in matching costs incurred and results produced—particularly when the results are not readily apparent, are not measurable in physical terms, and are evident only over a relatively long period

the difficulties of measuring the results produced by smaller units in terms of an organization's overall goals

the apparent impossibility of producing any one set of numbers useful for all purposes, and the confusion which this creates

and, finally, the ever-present tendency of individuals to distort information when results or plans would be adversely affected by the facts.

With a list of difficulties such as this, one could easily say that accountants have more than enough to do and should "stay home." Perhaps they should. There are, however, some compelling reasons for their not doing so—both in public and in self-interest. Let me suggest some of them.

1. Accountants are bothered that, even in business organizations where measurement is a relatively well-developed art, there are many important expenditures, usually made for a variety of "soft" purposes, which they find difficult to measure and evaluate. They recognize there is a strong possibility that the measurements which they now report in those areas are the ones which are easy to make and not necessarily the most useful ones. They recognize that, as business spends more for social purposes, managements are going to want to know more about whether the expenditures are productive and whether different types or amounts of expenditures might be more so. Accountants would like to be able to make intelligent response to these questions.

2. Accountants are deeply involved with governments, hospitals, housing authorities, schools—organizations which have as their *primary* purpose the direct achievement of some social objectives. Accountants realize that their usefulness in such organizations often falls short of their usefulness elsewhere and that the measurements they are making, because they relate to what can easily be measured, may be producing misleading indices of accomplishment and misallocations of resources.

3. Accountants reject the idea of "staying home" also because they think they have learned a good deal from what they have accomplished, and from the difficulties they have encountered, in their traditional arena. Some of this knowledge, they feel, would be useful in the development of social performance data, particularly when the task involves:

the development of economical, controlled systems for the ongoing accumulation of data

the creation of techniques for the integration of financial and non-financial data, and

the widespread communication of results.

4. Accountants have learned much about false and misleading information, about the conditions which produce it, and about the role of the auditor in providing reliability. If accountants and auditors are ultimately to attest social data to any substantial degree (as they already do in the case of some government grants and other special situations), they would like to help ensure that what they are asked to do—alone or in conjunction with other disciplines—is practical.

In short, accountants believe they know something about methods that work and those that don't work. They also feel that they and their clients could advantageously use a better measurement of social performance. They feel they have the resources to work simultaneously on their own accounting problems—formidable as they may be—and the newer problems of social performance measurement. And, finally, accountants feel that they have demonstrated on other occasions that they have an ability and a willingness to expand their knowledge into related fields when it is in their and the public's interest to do so.

Of course, just because accountants think they are good "counters" does not mean that they think their skills alone are enough. Under many circumstances, in fact, they would not even expect to be involved in the collection of data. And often, even when so involved, they would not claim to have the ability, which many of you have, to identify *what* it is that ought to be counted. Nor would they claim to know *how* to measure the particular phenomenon in all instances, for often the process of measuring will need the skill of the psychologist or the sociologist or a person with some other form of training. Nor, in many instances, would the accountant feel himself able to *interpret* results. You can be sure, however, that sooner or later the accountant will find himself increasingly involved, because sooner or later budgets, resource allocations, and reviews of results will be widely required. The more the accountant knows about the measurement of social performance, the more likely that his participation can be positive and productive.

I suppose one could say in summary that the accountant's interest rests on these premises:

The ability to determine the "state of society"—the costs and benefits of various efforts to improve it, and the costs of damages inflicted on it—is going to depend in the last analysis on the development of a sound measurement and reporting system. One can, for a time, get by with gross generalities. But, sooner rather than later, one will need more precise, agreed-upon measures if usefully specific evaluations, decisions, allocations of resources, and laws are to be made.

The accounting profession (and I include CPAs in public practice as well as those in industry, nonprofit organizations, and government) is concerned about measurement problems. This arises in part from the profession's substantial experience in data-gathering, attestation and reporting, and in relating financial and nonfinancial data. However, accountants by no means look on social performance measurement as a minor extension of their present activities; they know it is much more than that.

Accountants believe that it will, in most instances, be the function of other disciplines to decide what should be measured and, once measured, reported, and interpreted, but that they can contribute to developing measurement systems that are valuable to the user and yet practical from the standpoint of the producer. In the last analysis, any system will have to take into account the availability of data, the cost of their accumulation, the need to relate financial and social information, the ability to measure and report it, perhaps the need to audit it, and the ultimate requirement that macro and micro measurements somehow and to some degree be integrated and made consistent.

NAFTALIN: Is corporate involvement in matters of social measurement relating to the quality of life desirable? Should corporations be so involved?

MARLIN: Corporations *are* involved. We've no choice about that. My point is that they should be held accountable for their impact on the quality of life. The U.S. government and the investing, working, and consuming public should be provided with sufficiently precise and comparable information to form a basis for evaluation.

BIDERMAN: One element in Mr. Toan's remarks that I think it might be very profitable to discuss is the introduction of the certifying or attestation function into areas of social measurement. In the social field, the data are usually put up for grabs, as it were, for anybody to interpret, A notable development is the retaining of CPA firms by federal agencies to audit the statistical reports of recipients of government funds. The agencies want that information certified. We have examples of cases where statistics are used as the basis for award of government grants. There is a movement toward performance audits. It is an issue of "if" as well as "when" the certification function should be introduced into statistics.

BAUER: Audits of social actions are very hard to come by. The question of performance audits was raised. Essentially that means an audit to show whether the function that was intended is being carried out.

Let's take for example a lending program to black business. It can be attested to quite readily that a certain amount of money was shelled out and went to certain firms. But an audit probably doesn't tell me what I want to know. I want to be able to make some assessment of whether the program is going to work. One way of getting to that is asking the people responsible for it: "What's the logic of what you're doing?" I don't know what attestation is going to add to this, although it could perhaps describe the actions in sufficient detail to help make a decision as to whether the administrators' statement of theory or rationale was consistent with the facts.

DAVIDSON: Accountants are doing this sort of thing now in attesting to forecasts. They don't attest as to whether the forecast events will occur. They do attest to the logic underlying the forecast and whether the assumptions are reasonable.

CHURCHILL: I understand the GAO attests to the effectiveness and efficiency of the operations of government organizations as well as to the state of the financial reports.

MR. McELYEA: That's true. GAO for 10 years has been interested in this subject because Congress, as they consider requests for new appropriations, is constantly asking us for opinions as to how well managers performed with the resources provided in earlier years. And I can tell you that nothing is more frustrating than to audit, or try to audit, where there are no standards of performance. I assure you also that nothing is more dangerous than to go back to your employers year after year and say, "I can't tell." We are in that dilemma. I hope that we can devote time at this meeting to exploring how to begin an interdisciplinary development of standards which sociologists and educators and accountants and whoever else can use. Then we, as independent auditors, can look at the reporting and say, "Yes, that's the way it is," or report that we disagree and say, "They're not telling it the way it is." It seems to me somewhat unrealistic to be discussing here whether social programs are to be measured. I think measurement is inevitable. Mr. Nixon is reported to have said recently about the welfare program: "It's a mess." That's measurement of a sort, but it's not very useful for our purposes, nor is it enough for Congress to decide how and if the programs should be changed for the future.

LINOWES: We're talking about a new extension for the function of attestation. The financial audit, as we all know, is an attestation of a set of figures without comment as to whether a business is achieving its objectives or not. It simply determines whether the figures have been processed according to certain standards. But a possible variation might be, for lack of a better term, a socio-economic audit or, as the GAO puts it, a program audit. This should be conducted by an interdisciplinary team, perhaps captained by a CPA. A number of other disciplines should take part in determining whether or not an agency is accomplishing its purpose. I maintain that we already have those standards, but we aren't using them in this kind of an audit. In a welfare program, the program audit, the socioeconomic audit, could show that 10 million dollars was spent, and X number of people were made self-supporting. The same is true in penal institutions where a socioeconomic audit might show that in spending X dollars 120 people were rehabilitated—they have jobs and have now become contributing members of society. These are critical evaluations that are now missing from our budgetary and accountability processes, and yet these are elements which could be implemented almost overnight.

McELYEA: I'd like to say that 40 percent of the new people we now employ in GAO are not accountants; they are economists, sociologists, engineers, statisticians, actuaries. We don't have any psychologists yet.

WILSON: Reference has been made today to "norms." It seems to me that evaluation of the kind we're talking about now should be of a program's effectiveness against stated goals, whether we consider those goals as "norms" or not. In the national scope, norms are established through the political process. Except insofar as there are legislatively imposed norms, however, the specific institution's goals, whether it's a government agency or a business, are determined by the institution itself. You can then evaluate the progress made by that institution toward the self-imposed goals. There may well be very diffuse debate about the adequacy of these goals. I don't know if they will ever settle into norms of corporate performance. It seems to me it's going to be a constant dialogue process—a process of bidding and reacting. The corporation bids and says, in effect, "These are the goals we are adopting; we put them up for public display." And you then get a process of debate—a public evaluation of the adequacy of those goals. But I think if we wait for the establishment of norms, we aren't going to get off dead center. The way to begin is to begin.

McELYEA: I hope that's why we're here. We're likely all agreed with Art Naftalin that the final decision is political. But we're also agreed, I think, that in the matter of cost-benefit analysis we may be getting some bad answers because there aren't any very good rules for deciding what the costs are, or for deciding what the benefits are. And in the matter of choosing between alternatives it seems to me this is crucial.

MR. OLIPHANT: In accounting there has to be a certain amount of subjective reasoning and analysis. But there is also a great deal of objectivity involved and that's the basic role the accountant has studied to play. We dig out a lot more objective financial data today than in the past. I suggest what we feel is lacking is more objective social data. There is a tendency to the subjective when talking about social activity and social benefits because the norms are what someone thinks they are, and each of us may think differently about what the norms and standards are or should be. It seems to me, though, that we can determine what needs to be measured and how the different disciplines can coordinate efforts in performing that measurement, so we can end up with something a little more objective against which to measure actual events in the future.

McELYEA: The accountants have been busy for a couple of thousand years trying to help the businessman account for his bottom line.

What a terrific job is contemplated in attempting similar accomplishment in the social field!

OLIPHANT: That's right. We're accustomed to dealing with one segment and now, because of public expectation, government need, and so on, we're involved in a much broader sphere, and we don't know how to come to grips with it.

TOAN: Accountants can find many things besides norms with which to make meaningful comparisons, if by norm you mean something that is the one absolutely correct answer. Accountants compare present performance with the past; they compare actual expenditures with budgets; they compare the results of similar units; and so on. If more than one unit is trying to do the same kind of thing, they make inter-unit comparisons. So they find ways of measurement and approximation. And even if the measurements are not against norms, and the approximations are not exact to the last digit, the results are useful to the managers and decision-makers of an organization.

*After luncheon, to achieve easier give-and-take, the Roundtable was divided into two sections. One group was chaired by Professor Churchill.*

CHURCHILL: I suppose the best way of conducting this part of our meeting is to go around the table and let each person bring up questions or comments about the presentations and the discussion of them this morning. Bob, why don't you lead off?

PROF. BORUCH: The question was brought up by Mr. Bauer, Mr. Toan, and several others this morning as to the utility of the indicators. And I wonder whether one should talk about devising indicators without being able to evaluate their utility? I got no feeling from this morning's session of how to do it.

Toan: Social indicators should be useful in helping to establish the need for and objectives of programs, in choosing among alternative means of accomplishing given results, in determining the most appropriate level of expenditure, and in evaluating the results achieved. Indicators should have some utility in pinpointing problems, establishing priorities, telling us how well we're doing. They should have pragmatic value.

McElyea: May I say, too, that these standards or indicators, or whatever we call them, should enable outside persons to tell how well I'm doing as a manager. But it seems to me that the first necessity is for the manager himself to be able to tell, day-to-day, the extent to which he is attaining his objectives. Then the auditor, if you will, can come in and look at the record and attest to the reporting of it. The appraisal of results of social programs is almost always about entire large programs over long periods of time. There's not much available to tell the individual manager how *he* is doing day-to-day. This does violence to the way I think the management system ought to operate.

Naftalin: The two of you seem to be talking about the same thing— about the addition of auditing, evaluation, measurement—some dimension that is not now being observed. But is there sufficient similarity beween the measurement and auditing of ordinary business activities and measuring social activities to make a similar accounting?

McElyea: One way we can look at this is to attempt to associate costs with related benefits. In corporate accounting this process measures profit or loss, but in the public sector this is not yet so. We in the GAO have come to the point of view that there is not a great deal of difference, conceptually at least, in the attempt to associate the costs of the Head Start program, for example, with the benefits that it produces. Granted that it is something we accountants don't know how to do very well yet. Except in a very general way, managers haven't defined the benefits; certainly not to the point where a reading of progress can be obtained monthly, or even annually.

CHURCHILL: Art, was your question whether the indicators be the same for government policy as for business action?

NAFTALIN: I can see how the GAO might have an area of responsibility in which they are now asked to measure results. So a report is made using a set of standards. This then gets added to the financial audit. Is that it?

OLIPHANT: The semantics troubles me: "Audit" has a connotation in business that suggests a certain approach. I don't think it's really an audit we're talking about, but an examination or review, something other than an audit in the normal terms. After a review, just as after a systems review in a company, you could come up with suggestions or comments on the adequacy of the system. But that's not an audit; it's a review and a reporting on what's being done. I think a distinction should be made.

Aside from the question of review, we should be talking about standards of measuring. Otherwise, we're going to have different systems and need a translator. That's what happens in regulated industries today. Take, for example, requirements for reporting to the Federal Power Commission. The accounts are set up in a certain way which is useful to the Commission but, from a management point of view, is probably worthless. So there are two systems using the same data but subject to interpretation or translation.

TOAN: Wouldn't you also agree, Wally, that we're concerned about this kind of information being available to management, whether it's reviewed or audited or not?

OLIPHANT: Yes.

McELYEA: We've had a lot of difficulty over the years trying to get these terms straightened out. In our office we have a lot of roles—by statute we have a role as accountant; we're also engaged in auditing; we're engaged as advisers—you CPAs in public practice call this management advisory services. Perhaps it would help if we could clear up what the process of auditing is. I define it as the gathering of evidence about some activity and comparing the evidence to a standard of performance. This isn't unique to accountants. CPAS have always done this for financial statements. They are expert in that area and have a specific right—an exclusive right to express opinions on financial statements. But architects and engineers do something similar in comparing how a building is constructed with the plans. So it would help if we distinguish between accounting and auditing—I do not believe they are the same.

EISNER: I am puzzled by the implication of Art Naftalin's last question—whether we are speculating about the sorts of information business firms accumulate or about information a government or public body should put together in some way. We already have much in the way of social indicators—measurement of marriages, deaths, births, divorces. And much of our economic accounting already reflects a good bit of social activity. My own efforts are directed to extending economic accounting to include a great deal of information which is economically measurable. I don't know how much of that could or should be done at the corporate level, but I have some notions about how corporate accounts should be supplemented to make them more useful as a measure of economic performance, useful both for the firm and ultimately for the economy.

I am a bit puzzled as to precisely what we have in mind when we talk about the obligation of business firms or of accountants dealing with those firms to revise the accounts. We want some measure of when a corporation makes a contribution of benefit to society. Angus asked a question this morning about relating public benefits to private costs. I thought it was an apt question and I'm not sure he got a clear answer. Can anyone give it focus or are we just trying to give it focus as we discuss?

Much of what we are talking about can be expressed in economic terms—crime, for example, can be measured in terms of what happens to the property or human capital of the victim. I think one of the ways a lot could be contributed by accountants in their work for business firms would be measuring changes of value. To the economist, income is the total of what we can spend or consume plus the change in our net worth. But many changes in net worth are simply not reflected in income as now expressed in business financial statements or in income measure in our national accounts. So I think it would be a major contribution if we could come up with some way of having a supplement to the accounts that would reflect changes in values. In that way we could pick up a great deal of the social costs, external diseconomies, or, in some cases, the benefits, the economies, that are being created.

Beyond that there is a major need for a considerable extension of the national product accounts. Viewing the gross national product as the total of expenditures which do not represent a current charge by business and of government expenditures and private expenditures, we leave out a great deal and we include a lot which would not necessarily be a determinant of social and economic services.

CHURCHILL: Art, anything bother you about this morning?

TOAN: I want to come back to Dan Tunstall's description of the statistics which are being or will be accumulated and made generally available. I have some trouble in seeing how those types of statistics are going to be used to decide upon specific programs. I have even more trouble in seeing how those programs will later be evaluated by reference to the original set of indicators or measures or whatever it was that led to the decision to carry out the particular program in the first instance. In business, this circular process regularly occurs. There's feedback. In fact, the management cycle is often described as "Plan, direct, measure, control—re-plan, re-direct, re-measure, re-control." Clearly, measurement is a very significant part of that process. We, of course, find that this same cycle exists in some organizations concerned with social performance, such as hospitals, where the output can be fairly readily measured. However, there are many other entities devoted to social performance in which we don't see this process at work except in the most general terms. One of the reasons, I suspect, is that they or we haven't defined significant units of measurement—notice, I don't say standards of performance but units of measurement—and then succeeded in obtaining the relevant data.

CHURCHILL: Art Naftalin?

NAFTALIN: I guess I'm disturbed a bit that what we're referring to starts out with a large abstraction covering a multitude of diverse situations, and many of you feel we ought to arrive at some kind of procedure or format for filling in the abstraction. This troubles me because every situation I think of has so many variables and mysteries and unknown quantities that I don't know how to proceed in the specific situation, let alone in the general situation. It's kind of like talking in the academic field about a method for planning a curriculum. The notion of planning is quite difficult to encompass abstractly. I always retreat to, "O.K., I don't want to start out by thinking of planning as an abstraction. I want to think, for a while at least, about planning in this specific situation." In other words, proceed from a particular and go on to a series of particulars, and then I'll be ready to abstract from the series. Here we seem to be addressing ourselves to consideration of the abstraction without taking the time to define the particulars—which are hard to define even simply, let alone with regard to the complexities that emerge as you go along.

CHURCHILL: Walt Albers.

DR. ALBERS: What I would hope for from social indicators is that, not only at the national level but at the level of the individual company, they would identify some cause-and-effect relationships: if we change this here, we are going to be able to predict that effect there; or we see an effect there, and we have feedback to suggest that, by changing this cause, the effect will change in a direction profitable for society. We have a feeling that some cause-and-effect relationships can be extracted despite the complexities and the many variables. We now see a lot of conditions we'd like to change but we only speculate about causes. Yet we have some confidence that social indicators will be developed that we can use to test our models.

Why would we want social indicators without wanting to manage something? Is it too early in the social indicator search to answer the questions that have been raised here about utility? I have a firm conviction that the only way we're going to determine the utility of social indicators, and what we have to do to get them, is to jump in and start going. One may not have any firm idea of direction; whatever you do you're starting at ground zero. But as you develop work in some area on an ad hoc basis, you're going to gain experience, you're going to develop conceptualizations that you won't have by sitting back and debating. What I want to opt for is not to wait to identify what is ideal but to get started. Let's accept, by blind faith if necessary, that social indicators are going to be useful to us.

EISNER: Will you tell us what you mean by social indicators? Can you name one?

ALBERS: The victimization rate would be an indicator. Unemployment rates.

EISNER: Unemployment rates we have. Victimization rates . . .

ALBERS: Excuse me, I'm not sure that we have unemployment rates in the way that they're useful social indicators.

EISNER: Then you want to improve on the indicators we have.

ALBERS: Yes.

EISNER: All right, that's fine. But I don't know if that's the task for the CPAS.

CHURCHILL: Forget the CPAS. Who else?

CAMPBELL: There's a broad range of things that aren't being done now because nobody would pay for them. Eventually they probably will. If we are trying to think of things which are really indicators—something happening now that's going to give us some sense of what is going to happen six months from now—there probably aren't very many. I think we'd do better to talk of social *reporting*, social *measurement*, and get that indicator bit out of it. I can see how business feels it has to find some sort of return on every sort of investment and so would like that predictive value. But I would not like to see the federal government take that point of view. If it does, it seems to me the development of valuable series will be greatly delayed.

What I am saying is that the history of statistical series would probably indicate that a good many things get started without the prospect of immediate usefulness. They get started because there's some sense of impending need. There's the study by the Department of Labor, for instance, of how people evaluate their jobs. At the present time companies don't take that into account—whether the worker is happy on his job doesn't even get taken into consideration in bargaining on contracts with unions. The companies and the unions meet that by saying the job is a bad situation and the worker ought to get out of it as fast as possible. I believe, and some people in labor believe, that this attitude isn't going to last indefinitely—in the foreseeable future some union is going to say, "Look, that job is rotten. Either make it into a job a man can live with or give the man a premium for suffering through it—either by shortening his hours or doubling his pay."

TOAN: There already are pay differentials—for night work, difficult or dangerous working conditions, and other dissatisfactions. Maybe there are none for boredom or repetitiveness, but there is a long-standing concept of pay differentials for differences in working conditions.

CAMPBELL: That's right. The point I was making is that the federal establishment ought to gather some kinds of information not because the immediate translation into action is obvious but because it simply enlightens people about the state of society.

MCELYEA: As accountants, I don't think that anything said here so far should trouble us at all. I see us as being neutral, the standards as being neutral. On a yardstick, the 2 is no better or worse than the 12. What we'd like to think over with you social scientists is whether we can help you devise the means for gathering data that are relevant to what you are doing, which will help you, and whoever else to know how well you're getting along.

CAMPBELL: I would agree with Eisner that if you can gain new information by using data that are produced institutionally, and all you have to do is recast them, it's a lot better than having to go out and generate a lot of new data, especially by going to people and trying to get it out of them individually, which is very expensive. But I'm not satisfied with the implication of the example he used this morning that you assess people's satisfaction with their housing by counting the number who get so fed up that they move out. I wouldn't like to wait that long. I'd like to have some indications of that anger earlier in the game.

NAFTALIN: With respect just to government activities, we all know that they extend over a wide range, from highly specific, measurable activities to wholly indeterminate situations. For example, you might take an administrative activity such as the registration of motor vehicles and gather a lot more information. We might move to a much more complicated thing like the interstate highway system and examine its effects on industrial location, safety questions, spurs to the economy, social dislocations—20 or 30 things we'd want to know. Or farm subsidies. Some senator says, "These damn things, what have they done for us? What do the indicators show as to what we wanted the programs to do?" I'm not sure anybody knows what they want them to do, other than to get out of the production of some crop. Beyond this are all kinds of social problems—the whole question of who gets the benefits.

TOAN: I can appreciate the problems you mention, but I have difficulty in seeing how you would make a decision on such a matter without taking a number of factors into account in some weighted fashion. If you are going to do that properly, haven't you identified the relevant factors? You may not be at all sure you can measure them; you may have only a feeling about how important they are; you may not feel at all comfortable about delayed impacts, and so on.

But isn't much of the impetus for social measurement derived from a desire to substitute for vague feeling something a little more concrete?

NAFTALIN: In my view, every situation of social measurement involves some form of *a priori* standard, which will begin with political determination. I see the measurement activity as a series of discrete operations, each determined by the parameters set by political decision. I guess I just deny that there are universal standards that can be applied.

CAMPBELL: Something you said this morning made me think you felt that measurements had no relationship to social goals at all. But let's say we have a social goal to have a very low infant mortality rate. Now the fact that this is something we can measure, and the fact that the rate in the U.S. is higher than in several other countries puts pressure on our medical establishment to find out why it isn't better. To my mind, many social measurements have more value relatively than in the absolute. If you find that one part of the population as compared with another, or this country as compared to another country, has substantial differences or may be moving this way or that way, then you've got something that *is* relevant to programs for social action even though the data have nothing to do with setting absolute social goals.

OLIPHANT: Of course, comparative statistics on the same subject wouldn't help establish priorities as among different projects.

McCOMB: It seems that if we are going to make any progress on social measurement, it must be toward something to help us make judgments. Here you are at one point, and over here you are at another point, and you've either moved ahead or you're sliding back. Only with such information can we begin to see what kind of impact we are having, and the effects on society. It's like the census data—in 1969 you are still using the 1960 population data for New York City. Well, that is a good thing to know about 1960, but it doesn't help you really in 1969. Lacking a knowledge of the *change* that has taken place, we don't have the information we really need to make decisions.

BORUCH: Maybe in well-controlled environments like corporations, indicator systems can be direct and precise guide posts to action, but on the social level I'm not at all sure it's possible or desirable. For example, in the late 1950s someone studying data on arrests in New York discovered that the percentage of people for whom bail was not posted increased dramatically with the number of people arrested. They stayed in jail until their trials came up—the jails became more crowded. A problem was indicated. The data were there, but someone had to perceive their meaning: too many people, whose low income prevented them from posting bond, were languishing in jail. The statistics help one to perceive the problem, but they don't automatically point to a decision. That takes imagination, creativity, and, in some cases, an experiment.

In this case, someone suggested a large-scale experiment in which people who were arrested were randomly assigned to two groups—in one they had to post bond, and in the other they didn't. The Vera Institute of New York City actually did the experiment early in the 1960s, with the cooperation of New York judicial administrators and with Ford Foundation funds. The objective was to determine if it was posting bond that led people to show up for trial, or something else. It turned out that for a very large group of arrests for felony, misdemeanors, and other offenses, where bail was eliminated, people did show up for trial. The only people who lost out were the bail bondsmen. Presumably, society gained in some sense. People whose incomes were low were at least out working pending trial, contributing to the GNP. My point is that social indicators are a sort of building block to begin with. When you talk about the utility of social indicators, that's really a function of the kind of organization you've got. Corporate enterprises might take a systems approach that would lead to decisions. Presumably, the process is facilitated because the linkage between indicators and consequences is so close in a well-controlled environment such as some corporations or some physical phenomena. In other kinds of enterprises, I'm not so sure the linkage is at all strong. And even after perception of a problem through use of indicators, you have to have the ability to develop a strategy of solution.

EISNER: Taking the example of Mr. Boruch's remarks, you can see that ultimately value does attach to these measurements. Earlier Art Toan mentioned the problem of weighting. We have lots of economic statistical series which can be taken as a measure of something social but which we have not interpreted in this way. One difficulty in using them is to know how to weight them. For example, some economic statistics, considered as unquestionable in terms of politics, really aren't. People are *not* agreed that we should have zero unemployment. Maybe a lot of people don't like to admit it, but there are many economists who think the economy functions better if there is some unemployment. It increases productivity, decreases inflationary pressures.

I suggest that economic current accounts, which we already have, can go a long way toward providing a set of systematic values to things that are not economic. Take the example of the arrests and bail bonds—there's an economic question here. The bare statistic of non-bonded people who did show up—let's say 98 percent—still doesn't give you all the answers. What you would like to know is: what values are to be placed on what they did with their time not spent in jail? This could perhaps be ascribed to whatever they earned, whatever values the market put on their services. From that you want to subtract the cost of chasing down the 2 percent who didn't show up. You might also have to subtract the cost to society of whatever crimes were committed by the 2 percent. There's a whole set of things to add, to subtract, and to put values on.

I've sometimes thought that when people talk of the need for social indicators they really mean a systematic program of measurement which comes out with a number at the bottom, by which we could attribute values. Otherwise, we're left with a whole set of numbers we don't know what to do with. Economists often face this problem— you have unemployment of 6 percent and price inflation of 6 percent; now what does it mean? Do you want to reduce unemployment to 5 percent and let inflation go to 7 percent? How do we balance these two? Economists haven't yet put together weights that tell us whether we're socially better off or worse in the alternative circumstances.

CHURCHILL: I wouldn't argue that economics should not be part of the decision-making process. But I'm not sure that the start for social indicators is economic. Take pollution—economic measures rarely dealt with it because you just passed it on down the stream. Now the debate is: is it cheaper to clean it at the source or cheaper to let the company dirty the water and then clean it up downstream? Now you're in an economic venture. But until you start to develop measures of pollution and consideration of the system rather than just one plant on just one river, it is not a corporate economic venture in any classical sense.

EISNER: It should be. The difficulty, as I suggested earlier, is macro economics, the Gross National Product, the total expenditures which are not charged to current accounts by business. That's a very narrow view of measuring output. There's a great deal of output in the household, a great deal of output by government, that simply doesn't get counted. There's also a great deal of negative output—the destruction of capital—which we don't count. And yet I think income and product accounting can go a long way. I think the huge gap now existing in business accounts is that we don't mention any change in the value of property. A firm may spend hundreds of millions on R & D, and it doesn't show up as an increase in the value of the firm. On the other hand, if it spends hundreds of millions buying plant and equipment that turn out to be obsolete, it still shows up as a big increase in the value of the firm.

CHURCHILL: Temporarily. At least, there is no reduction in value.

EISNER: Capital is something that will produce income in the future. The stock of knowledge derived from research and development can affect the future just as surely as plant and equipment will. We have no adequate measure of education because we don't recognize that it's an investment in human capital. Investments in human capital can be valued, and if you don't value them you're really short in your measure of the stock of capital. Is it true that we're wasting a lot of money on education as the Coleman report may be taken to suggest? How would you know?

I think the main constraints on business should be the market, but there are many instances where the market cannot function as constraint because of what we keep calling external economies. The market obviously doesn't influence General Motors or any individual car-buyer to worry about polluting the atmosphere; the pollution I create won't make the slightest bit of difference, so there's no sense in my buying a small car or an electric scooter if millions of other Americans are going to buy polluting cars.

ALBERS: But, in general, business cannot perceive a constraint until society identifies it and indicates that business should be concerned about it.

EISNER: No, society shouldn't just tell them to be concerned; society—through government—should tell them exactly how to be concerned, as by prohibition, with legal penalties or by a tax program. I think we have to come to some kind of balance between private cupidity on the one hand and vigilantism on the other. That is, you have a sort of race between business firms anxious to make the most money and get away with what they can and self-appointed custodians of the public good who try to frighten them out of making the money.

McCOMB: Let me pose an example that may be pertinent. In our business we're developers of shopping centers, and this involves going out and buying land, and perhaps ten years after you've bought the land you actually start pouring concrete and developing a center. By then the metropolitan planners have identified the shopping center as being what they call a major diversified center. This has become an element of public policy. The public agencies then become involved in trying to ascertain what types of activities should be taking place in such a center—on land that is owned by a private company. We realize that the centers we're building today may not meet the expectations of people ten years from now. Now is it part of our social responsibility to try to determine what kind of center we should be building ten years from now? We have to involve the sociologists, planners, and other experts to develop that type of center. We must have a rationale for going to that community and saying, "Here's what we want to build and here's what we think it's going to do for this community." All of the practical considerations that make the center an economically viable venture must be included. If the project doesn't generate a profit, there will not be a shopping center—unless the government gets into the business, and we haven't come to that point yet. We have to undertake this type of planning if we're going to be in the development business ten years from now. I don't know if this is social responsibility or just long-range planning.

EISNER: It's long-range planning. I don't see any social responsibility there. You say you have to do this to keep in business; that's fine. Your consideration is your stockholders.

ALBERS: How about the consumer?

EISNER: You have to satisfy the consumers to sell your products and make money for your stockholders. The community has a right and an obligation to establish restrictions (where the marketplace itself does not) sufficient to ensure the social good. They may want to zone you out of a particular area because, while it's optimum for you to have a shopping center there in terms of making money, there will be greater loss in terms of value of houses and other attributes of the neighborhood.

ALBERS: This isn't the problem we started to address. The problem is why business is motivated to get into the social indicator business. We've avoided that question. Aren't we trying to identify the motivation?

CAMPBELL: Bob, you told me at lunch that a company gives money to charity for reasons of public relations, and to avoid downtown boycotts and similar nuisances. It's to its economic advantage to buy that off, so to speak. Why can't GM or anybody else argue: If we don't spend this money to satisfy the public and show public interest and so on, the legislators down in Lansing will enact some regulation that's the last thing in the world we want. So, with long-range planning, we will make this expenditure now because we want to avoid something 10 or 20 years from now.

EISNER: You have suggested what I think it often comes down to: a show as a substitute for effective action.

CAMPBELL: Maybe that's no more reprehensible than an individual's giving to the United Fund.

EISNER: Giving to the United Fund is a bit the same thing, a matter of assuring goodwill.

CHURCHILL: Charles Abt maintains he can walk into a company and save them 10 percent of their social overhead. He says that the decisions made on allocating dollars to employee benefits and well-being are badly misspent. We haven't made adequate measurement of what employees really want. What's the tradeoff between the bowling alley and the nice cafeteria? Or the basketball team and the bus service? That's a social measurement that hasn't been made very often. But it comes down to an influence on the bottom line of profit and loss providing more that the employees desire for equal or less money.

McCOMB: Based on my experience, a businessman who sees a social problem may search for a way to use corporate resources to solve the problem. So then you get into utilizing corporate resources to solve social problems. I don't think it's a case of our coming to such a conclusion out of consideration of self-preservation.

EISNER: You know, what you're saying is that we should let a hand-ful of people, a company's board of directors, decide how to run society. They have the money and they should decide what's good. I don't see that at all. They may be wiser, I admit, than a lot of other people, but they have their own points of view, their own attitudes, and there's no particular reason to trust them to deal with social prob-lems. That's the wrong way to go about it.

Suppose they decide the way to handle the deterioration of Detroit is to keep all the blacks out. They decide this very conscientiously and conclude that the races just can't mix well and that mixing causes all kinds of trouble. And they then begin using their money for propa-ganda, an educational program, subsidies. You keep thinking of them doing things that you and I happen to agree with, but there are many things they might do that I don't agree with.

ALBERS: But it doesn't appear to work that way. Rather, social de-mand identifies what the problems are.

EISNER: If it's in their economic interest, they should be permitted to do whatever they wish. But if in our political judgment there's some social disinterest to what they are doing, then we may prohibit them from doing it or tax them for doing it. But whatever they can do for their own benefit, I'm willing to have them do. You see, you would have a few people, the members of a board of directors acting as individuals, decide what's good for society with no regard for what's good for the corporation.

MCCOMB: Don't forget that I said they would use their resources to solve a problem. . . .

EISNER: A problem for whom?

MCCOMB: It could be a problem for the city, it could be a problem for the corporation.

EISNER: Why should they use corporate resources to solve a problem for the city?

CAMPBELL: On the argument of long-term planning. On the argument that, if they don't do it, the city is going to pass an ordinance that is going to cramp them. I think that's a very important point you raise, Bob, that if the corporate management undertook to spend money on social programs we thought were undesirable, we would certainly disapprove. But I don't believe that's a completely constructive argument, because there must be a handful of social goals, like reducing the infant mortality rate, which nobody can argue with, and there must be plenty of places where industry can put money of this kind, and I'm persuaded that they should.

EISNER: Let's go back to Detroit—I can build an example around that. One of the problems is that there are very few people living in downtown Detroit. Everybody has gone to the suburbs. Everybody is generally agreed there should be more housing there and that it should be low, middle, high income and it should be well done. Hudson's could say we're going to ignore that or we're going to pitch in and help. And I don't see anything wrong in the corporation's saying, okay we're going to utilize corporate resources to help the community.

I suggest one utility of social measurement is as a source of information to help a corporate management make decisions which are good for the company itself. If saving downtown Detroit is what's good for the company, for example, that's what they're going to try to do. Now that takes a lot of information, more than we have on hand at present. Most people would agree that General Motors is a pretty successful corporation, making decisions largely on information of a technological nature. They couldn't possibly have grown and survived as they have without an excellent system for gathering and developing and evaluating technological information. One has to start developing a comparable and complementary system for gathering social information. We don't know where to start or how best to utilize such social information as we have. There's your problem from the business point of view.

CAMPBELL: It strikes me that a primary difference between a corporation and the United States government is that the corporation is likely to have some local base. The government can't really respond to community problems very well, so it seems to me that's precisely the focus that a company ought to have. If I were on the board of one of your companies, I would be concerned with what I could learn about the community where my plant is, where my employees are.

TOAN: You didn't include the communities where your products are sold. Was that intentional?

CAMPBELL: No, it was not. I didn't include them because it didn't occur to me.

TOAN: If your products are cars, you will cover a lot of the country—in fact, a good part of the world.

MCELYEA: We're not talking about just federal government. There are many other levels of government where they can deal with local problems—where we locate plants, how we pollute a stream, how we live with the community around us.

EISNER: My own research efforts at present are directed at helping devise a system of keeping product accounts that would include all consumption and all capital accumulation or loss of capital values. We'd be measuring, for example, production in the household by household workers including housewives; we'd be measuring the capital accumulation of government, the plant and equipment, highways and so forth, and the services of this capital which would include the income from capital and charges for depreciation, even though we don't measure that currently. We'd be measuring the accumulation of human capital and the loss of human capital and that, I think, should pick up a great many things that sociologists and social psychologists and most of us are interested in obtaining. We'd want to know the increase in human value from educational expenditures, from being brought up properly in the home, with both parents; we'd want to know the loss in values from broken homes, crime, disease. I have in mind a comprehensive set of accounts for all changes in capi-

tal value, including human capital. Then, although it might be difficult to work out precisely how, we could conceivably pick up the
effects—the measured effects not the subjective effects—of so many
things that concern us. Even the non-physical things people have—
how much do they reflect themselves in some measure of values and
the income they can earn?

To go back to business concerns and the question of the disameni-
ties of a job, one question would be how much more, or less, people
would work if the job were made more pleasant. Suppose GM conducted an experiment and said, "We'll give you eight dollars an hour
for this crummy, monotonous job the way it is, but we're willing to
have music piped in to make the job less monotonous, and so forth.
But you realize this will cost money, and therefore we can only pay
you seven-fifty an hour." One question is, how many workers would
take the seven-fifty?

Justin Davidson remarked that students complain they want smaller
classes, yet at his school a class meeting at nine a.m. has 200 students
sign up for it, while another class meeting at one p.m. has 20. Students don't like registering for classes in the afternoon, and that
gives you a notion of the relative value they put on small classes. We
would look for values of this kind and try to relate economic values
to some total system of accounts that doesn't leave us saying: "Gee,
pollution! Let General Motors spend a hundred dollars more per car
to abolish pollution." That's no good; you have to have some kind
of measure. The self-appointed custodians of the public good don't
really take into account what the costs are relative to the benefits, and
they're not providing the measures for them.

ALBERS: In my opinion, that's what we are at least hoping to do. It's
on faith that such measures can be developed.

TOAN: You say "on faith." I would say faith and logic and a certain
amount of experience. I think it's far more than on the basis of faith.

ALBERS: By that I mean, the decision to invest the large amounts of
time and resources necessary rests largely on faith in the outcome and

to a much smaller degree on experience and logic. We are at the beginning of social measurement; we don't have the fact of social measurement. I was under the impression that our purpose here these few days was more to identify how to make the start so that our hosts would have a feeling for what they should begin to think about in terms of their role—not so much discussing social measurement as an existing, ongoing part of business operation, but rather looking forward to its being that some day.

*Concurrent with the session chaired by Professor Churchill, a second group was led in discussion by* DEAN DAVIDSON.

DAVIDSON: This morning was marked by divergent views, and I expect we'll have more this afternoon. Let me talk briefly about what I hope we can accomplish. I suggest that we focus on two questions. First, what are the main problems in the social measurement area, the things each of you thinks are so important that they should be attacked promptly? Second, what sort of commonalities are there in these problems? In one sense this thing called social measurement is like the elephant that the blind men came to explore. I'd like to see if we can agree on the overall form of the elephant. One way of going about this is to go around the table and ask each of you what you think are the one or two main problems. Then perhaps we can come back and discuss commonalities of the problems that have been raised. I'll start on my left with Lee Brummet.

PROF. BRUMMET: Rather than being directly responsive to your suggestions, Justin, I may yield to the temptation to say a few things I thought to say this morning but wasn't aggressive enough to get in. My label really doesn't indicate what my background is—I guess I'm an accountant. I couldn't help thinking this morning what might have been the justification for a meeting like this. There is a possibility that the accountants think they have something to contribute to the work of the social scientists and invited them here to listen to their expertise. Or it might be the reverse, that the accountants need help and think they might learn from the political and social scientists. I believe the most justified point of view is that this is an area that absolutely requires joint effort. I think accountants are justified in feeling that by their training and involvement they have developed an entrée to the businessman and business thinking which may exceed that of the social scientists, and that, if we are looking at the social impact that changes in attitudes and objectives of businessmen might have, the accounting route has something to offer. Also, I think the accountants are justified in believing they have expertise in systematizing information flows and even in the possibility of inferential kinds of interpretation, while the social scientists have more expertise in social measurements themselves. So these are grounds for a natural cooperative effort.

There is more commonality in this field than we generally recognize as we ply our trades and our interests on a rather separate basis. One observation about this morning: I have a bit of difficulty with the attempt to separate measures into "hard" and "soft" data, or objective and subjective data. I think these dichotomies tend to confuse more than to simplify the issues. We in the accounting field use some pretty soft measures and come up with figures that look terribly hard. I wondered about several references—by Art Toan, as I recall, and I see he's not with this group—to "hard facts." We do not have many "hard facts." If you take a 100 percent sample of the population, perhaps you get some hard facts, but even there we have perceptions of facts rather than hard facts themselves. We are really dealing with symbolic representation of phenomena. Some representations may be pretty good and some may be pretty bad. Let me suggest the kind of framework I would like to think in.

Some of the comments this morning were about social measurement at the micro level within profit-making organizations and nonprofit organizations, and some were at the macro level. I think that accountants can be most effective in the business sector. They can assist in developing social measures that can be used for planning, directing, and appraising social programs. This would assist managers in making the decisions they want to make in terms of their announced objectives. It would also assist in the decisions of the investing public, those individuals who control the movement of economic resources. It would give the investor a chance if he wants to invest in a socially conscious organization. We don't know if he will, but we should give him a chance. At the moment he doesn't have that chance because he is told a certain kind of information but not another kind that is at least as significant. In this area it seems to me there are two possibilities—one is to mount an effort to change the thinking as to the content of this thing we call net income or profit.

Eisner was talking this morning (why is it I keep referring back to people who didn't get into this group?)—Eisner was talking about profit maximization. He had to be talking, it seems to me, about the numbers that accountants call profits. But those numbers are not what the economist would call profits. They are not what the sociologist might like to call profits, especially if the numbers do not include some representation of social impact. So I think there's some progress to be made by weaving into the profit measurement some of these factors. One of the big advantages of doing so is that the information would be in the form with which the businessman is already familiar.

But I don't think we should limit our efforts there. There are other things to be done. Dave Linowes emphasizes, for example, a sort of socioeconomic report in addition to the usual financial report. When we come to the nonprofit organizations, we have made very little progress in the measurement of outputs, let alone of the social factors involved. These are areas we should pursue.

Then as to the macro level, it seems to me that social indicators can be derived only in part by an additive process of social indicators in business; it's something more than that. These strike me as important aspects of our subject.

DAVIDSON: I would like to let everyone react to each speech. But if we're to get all main views, I'd better let everyone speak in order. I turn now to Mrs. Marlin.

MARLIN: I'd like to take this opportunity to tell you more about the Council on Economic Priorities. It is a non-profit research organization that has, for the last two and a half years, been evaluating the performance of major U.S. corporations on a comparative basis in areas such as employment, promotion and training of minority group members and women or installation of pollution control equipment. We've also listed their contracts for military production. We've done a few comparative analyses of corporate involvement in South Africa. We may in the future be analyzing corporate involvement in developing countries too.

We've just completed a 14-month evaluation of the efforts of 15 electric utilities at installing the best pollution control equipment available. This is our second in-depth environmental study, following our 1970 study of the pulp and paper industry, to be published, with a 1972 update, by MIT Press. Each depth study is updated periodically. In the case of the paper study, the improvements in the two intervening years have been dramatic: in 1975, the 24 companies studied will have installed the best pollution control equipment available at virtually all of their pulp mills, and in 1973 five will have achieved first-rate control, compared with only two in 1970.

In each study we begin by educating ourselves about the production processes, pollutants, and possible ways to control them with commercially available equipment. We investigate the cost of installing this equipment, and examine each major plant operated by a company to ascertain whether adequate equipment has in fact been installed. We obtain general background information from secondary sources like scientific and trade journals and technical books dealing with the subject, as well as government publications. We talk with the staffs of pollution control companies and government agencies. We check on the legal status of each plant with the relevant state pollution control officials. Then we design highly detailed questionnaires and check them with established experts in the field—scientists, industrialists and environmentalists—who act as our advisors on a pro bono basis because they consider our work important and its quality good.

Only once we've assured ourselves that we're asking the right questions does the most delicate and difficult aspect of our work begin. We write to each company and telephone them soon afterwards, seeking their extensive cooperation in providing us with data and granting us interviews with their environmental experts. Our record of success varies. In the case of the paper industry, 22 of the 24 companies contacted cooperated extensively in providing us with the requisite data. This high proportion of cooperative companies was obtained only after months of cajoling and careful explanation of our objective approach and technical competence. Interestingly, when the press reported on our findings, its heaviest criticism was not of the companies with the worst records, though these were certainly heavily criticized. The most adverse commentary was reserved for the companies that refused to discuss their efforts with us honestly. It seems the public can understand failure to comprehend early the full impact of the environmental crisis at hand, or the lack of adequate funding to install the best control equipment available, or even the lack of technical competence to select the best equipment and make it work, but the public cannot sympathize with a refusal to disclose information, to discuss problems fully and openly. The public objects to corporate secrecy on social issues.

The point clearly struck home at the paper companies. In the 1972 update, both the previously uncooperative companies provided the Council with extensive information and were in fact anxious to discuss their problems and records with our researchers.

In the case of the utilities study, every company approached has cooperated fully. While one reason may be the fact that extensive information about the utilities is on file at the Federal Power Commission, the existence of detailed information in the permit applications of steel companies to the U. S. Army Corps of Engineers has not deterred the steel companies from refusing adamantly to provide the Council with even skeletal data.

One of the most interesting studies to be based on Council findings is the Bragdon-Marlin study, which compared the pollution control performance of the paper companies with their profitability. They expected that companies which spent money on pollution control would at least at first suffer financially. They found that the best pollution-controllers were the most profitable companies. One might expect that only already profitable firms could afford to install the requisite equipment. But Bragdon and Marlin found that the two cleanest companies had begun to install their excellent equipment long before they became profit leaders and that the largest company in the industry, now lagging in profitability, had failed to install good control equipment when it was a profit leader. The authors' conclusion is that both good earnings and good pollution environmental records flow from good management.

The vacuum of data in the social area is staggering. Try to imagine what it would be like to do financial analyses of an industry and the largest 30 companies in it without any of the existing sources of information, like registration forms at the SEC, annual reports, investment banking and brokerage house reports, Standard & Poor's, Moody's or other conventional reporting organizations and analytical work. That's the position we're in now.

Our studies are summarized in our bi-monthly *Economic Priorities Reports*, which has 3000 subscribers.

TANNENBAUM: When you're investigating what it would cost to install the best pollution controls, do you also investigate the possible consequences like changes in rate structures, the price rises that companies often attribute to outlays for pollution abatement?

MARLIN: Only in some cases. We always investigate what it would cost each company to install the best pollution controls. In some cases, like the utilities study, we can estimate the cost to the consumers. For utilities, the cost per kilowatt hour is provided.

LINOWES: I'm one of the 3,000 subscribers to your *Economic Priorities Report*. The question that has come into my mind several times is where you get your data, where does the input come from? I can't help feeling sometimes that I want to question the source of the base material. I'm wondering what disciplines help contribute to your report. The report itself fills a void, but I often feel uncomfortable because I don't know where you're getting these statements and judgments.

MARLIN: The *Economic Priorities Reports* are different from the full in-depth studies and are not meant for business use. If you have sufficient interest to order the in-depth studies, you'll find they're very carefully footnoted and that all data are painstakingly attributed. Perhaps we should put more footnotes in the *Economic Priorities Report*, but usually the general public isn't interested in the sources of our information. People who have greater or more technical interest should order the in-depth study.

BRUMMET: Do you have any indication as to what use the security analysts put this to—what they infer from it or how they feed it into their appraisals?

MARLIN: I can't speak for them, but they seem to be primarily interested in knowing if it's a valid assumption that government regulations are going to become more strict, whether agencies are becoming more efficient in enforcement. They want to know which companies are most vulnerable—how much they're going to have to spend—which companies have planned well in advance and are going to be well-positioned so that they're not going to be subject to attacks by community groups and sued.

DAVIDSON: You're next, Chuck.

MR. SCARLOTT: Trying to make a contribution from a business perspective here, I think I'll attempt a quick commentary on the elements of the corporate role—not to precipitate a discussion of what the corporate role should be but to give some idea of where, in my view, a business could most particularly benefit from improved information.

I guess it's not uncommon to suggest that business responsibility can be divided into three basic levels. The first and foremost is to do its economic job well, which itself has highly important social value. Second, to discharge that activity with a high degree of sensitivity to social effects. And third, to reach out beyond the basic business functions, to identify and support more general objectives—for example, education, the arts, and so on.

Now, looking at these levels of responsibility, I would tend to agree with Professor Eisner that if we get too ambitious about the role of business we will diminish economic efficiency and very possibly end up with a net *loss* in social value. Some of these social goals are very poorly defined, much less agreed upon. Many are inherently hard to quantify or to get agreement on. Until there is more concrete agreement about social objectives and standards, there is a high risk of individual boards of directors making inept and/or conflicting decisions—personal and idiosyncratic decisions—that don't fundamentally contribute toward a solution of key social problems. Moreover, I am personally somewhat skeptical at this point about the feasibility of social accounting in terms of financial statements.

From the standpoint of what business should do, it seems to me the most immediately constructive measurements would be those leading to better understanding of the social consequences or costs of businesses' "normal" commercial operations. In the industry in which my company is engaged—oil—pollution is a problem. This is a subject on which the industry obviously has a great deal of knowledge, and it can—must—make a major contribution toward solutions. But we would certainly be serving the economy poorly if we were to set or lightly accept a goal of, say, zero pollution. In the first place, a pollution-free environment is probably an impossibility since nature itself creates a lot of pollution, as human beings generally conceive the term—emissions from volcanoes and swamps, smoke from forest fires, silting of streams, natural eutrophication, and so on. Second, to achieve absolute purity would require an allocation of resources that would almost certainly be disproportionate in the light of socially attractive alternative uses of such resources, which are not unlimited.

From our industry's point of view, pollution is unquestionably problem No. 1. Beyond that, I think for industry as a whole—that is, industry outside the service area—a better measurement of the consequences of pollution on the one hand and, on the other, of the all-in costs of control, is a most fruitful area in which to look for improved measurement. I think business itself should accept a responsibility to be more forthcoming and cooperative in developing and sharing this information.

I am using pollution only as one example. But what I want to make clear also is that I doubt that many of the areas we have been talking about today—crime, health, education—are things that should be left primarily or even significantly to business. Even where business does something about these matters, I doubt it can handle them effectively in the absence of explicit guidelines clearly defined by government to facilitate a rationally organized and equitably distributed effort. Better measurement systems should facilitate *intelligent* harnessing of business to a gradually widening role. But the thrust of my remarks was to say—what is business equipped to do, by competence and political mandate? The best way for business to make a contribution is by starting in its own backyard before it volunteers itself into other poorly charted areas.

DAVIDSON: Are you saying there is a crying need for some of these measurements, but that you don't think business is the proper one to take the lead?

SCARLOTT: I'm saying business is poorly equipped to appraise—or even measure—the social utility of what it does, apart from guidance received from the commercial marketplace and from the political process. I am defining the role for the corporation as limited and primarily economic. In the execution of its economic role business should be as sensitive as it can to the social consequences. But don't expect it to be ahead of society in this regard. I think it is unrealistic to expect business to conduct basic research to find out what these social consequences are.

TANNENBAUM: What do you think of the idea of imposing taxation on industry to finance research in some areas, such as pollution?

SCARLOTT: If uncertainty exists as to the social effects of economic activities, it appears reasonable for society to take the lead in exploring the uncertainty. But, as I think I said earlier, I do agree that industry should help finance the research in some manner. I see no objection to society's imposing regulation or taxation based on adequate research. Where the research needs are very large, no one company can conduct the research on its own; moreover, the antitrust laws will prevent companies from getting together to do it. Perhaps the antitrust laws should be re-examined in this particular respect.

BAUER: I take it you feel that one of the most important uses for a system of social measurement would be to help corporations make more orderly decisions with respect to their social programs. This, I think, would include experiments on forms of display of measurements, so that executives could sit down and look at some numbers and make sense out of them and work with them. I feel that there is a great need for just plain orderliness.

SCARLOTT: I think executives do need a better display of the social consequences of their companies' activities than can be obtained by working some kind of new data into financial statements. It seems unlikely that there will be developed very soon a statement which somehow blends financial data with nonfinancial data. I am not sure it's all that attractive to try to construct such statements as opposed to finding other means—quantitative where possible but not necessarily financial—for understanding the social consequences. I agree that more, and better organized, knowledge is essential to good decision-making. Concerning business reaching out beyond its economic role, I was interested in the remark by one of our number this morning that he is charged with improving the quality of life of the inner city. Such a person must certainly have a desperate need for better measures of what life is like in the inner city, what it reasonably can be, and what the net, not simply the immediate, consequences of given corporate actions are likely to be, with the state of the art as it is today. I would be terribly inadequate to execute such a grandiose charge.

LINOWES: I differ with the idea that it is impossible for business to take leadership in helping to solve some of the critical problems of our cities. At present I'm chairman of the City Affairs Committee of the New York Chamber of Commerce, which has been doing some very effective work in training and hiring hard-core unemployed. Several hundred people have been trained, and the participating corporations have hired them as they were trained. These corporations include some of the biggest in the country. In this activity we see important executives putting in time, money, and effort, and having wholesome, beneficial results in some difficult areas of the City of New York, such as Harlem.

Another social problem our group is attacking is recidivism in ex-convicts. The recidivism rate is about 80 percent. This committee of business executives is now spearheading an effort to improve training programs in prisons, to prepare inmates for employment outside. The effort is to bring the training program in prison up to a level equivalent to that within industry.

Here I have mentioned two important voluntary efforts by business that are working, are effective, and the people taking part in them are the hardest-headed types of business executives.

SCARLOTT: I don't see that what you describe runs counter to what I have in mind. I said companies could do so much more in their own backyard, but I didn't think their prime social responsibility is to take leadership in attacking social problems generally, or in research on measurement for setting standards on those matters. The business executives you speak of are the type of individuals we need more of. But I don't think that we are going to lick the underlying problems of the society—and they are massive, interconnected, and abstruse— with the kinds of undertakings you mention. Experience in such efforts so far is that the results taper off rather quickly, far short of what is needed. There is in such activity a tendency to pick around the edges of the problems.

There is also a danger that if too much reliance is put on voluntary programs, there will be a backlash of discouragement when they prove to be not effective. The problem of the hard-core unemployed may be an example.

TANNENBAUM: My own inclination is not to be so terribly enthusiastic, and not to feel overly optimistic about such organizations set up by businessmen to do this sort of thing. The simple fact is that corporations are not organized for this purpose. It does not hurt when they try it, but neither should we expect solutions from such activities.

Beyond that, I think social indicators are still a long way off. They are not readily forthcoming, and until they are, we run the risk of acting on the basis of measurements of one kind or another just because they are available—because they seem to give us a handle on something—but not necessarily valid. In some areas, the available measure may be quite useful. But in other areas, like education, the ambiguity of goals is such as to cause considerable problems of interpretation and the like. Under such circumstances, we run the risk of thinking that just because we can get a measure, we can do something with it regarding policy, funding, and so on. Scores on reading tests, for example, have become a goal in and of themselves, and not necessarily because they provide a valid index of a desired performance. There are performance contracts where, if the students in a school class reach a certain pre-established goal on the test, as such, you get a fixed amount of money in return, without much assurance of actual improvement in the knowledge and ability the test is supposed to measure. This is the use of operational definition in the extreme and invites all sorts of obvious tautologies.

My suggestion, then, is to be patient at the present time, rather than run the risk that the cure may be worse than the disease. There is evidence of such premature action in the field of pollution, for example. I don't know what the present view is on the presence of phosphates in detergents, but it is apparent that the attitude has changed in a relatively short period. There were government rulings that brought in substitute materials that have proved to be worse than the ones they replaced. Accordingly, I am skeptical of quick solutions to long-standing problems.

For that matter, I am not sure that this is the time to have a conference such as the present one. As I look at the different aspects of problems that have been brought up, I think it is clear we are going to have to develop different measurements in different areas rather than a general set of measurements. In the area of pollution, for example, not only do we not know what solutions are possible, we are far from certain as to how to approach the problem in the first place, despite all the current talk. I am told that the smog problem in New York is worse now as compared to 1935, but lacking adequate measurements then and now, I am not sure this is really so.

Similarly, are we prepared to face the costs involved in some of the currently trumpeted changes? There are going to be costs in reducing the pollution effects of automobiles and making them safer. If an average automobile is going to cost $8,000 in terms of today's dollar, what's the effect going to be?

TUNSTALL: I don't agree we should proceed as slowly as you suggest. There are many areas in which we are capable of making judgments right now. We have information adequate for making public and corporate policy. There are many types of pollution about which we know a great deal. By taking action, and making mistakes and receiving criticism, we learn. A good set of quality indicators results from mistakes and criticism.

[VOICE]: In response to your effort, Percy, to move the talk away from corporate responsibility to social indicators, it seems to me the two are closely tied together—that measurement at the micro level is just as important to the idea of indicators as measurement at the macro level—maybe more so. I can imagine, for example, developing some criteria we might think were pretty good as social indicators but still having no information as to the extent to which, say, a changed government policy such as taxation or subsidization would affect those indicators and cause them to show whether we are enjoying higher quality of life. If we can get measurements at the corporate level as well as on the macro level, we have a better chance of sensing some cause-and-effect relationships rather than just measuring whether life is getting better or some random kind of thing is taking place we can't identify.

TANNENBAUM: Regarding the so-called quality of life, my preference is against general measures applied to all people across all areas of social activity. I am far from convinced that I want someone else's idea of quality of life imposed upon me. About the sole criterion I can accept at this time is that of maximizing my choice—my own choice as a distinct individual—in a great variety of areas. Any trend in the direction of maximizing available choice is desirable to me as a social goal, but beyond this I am not sure whether accelerated growth, or zero growth, or even retarded growth in a given activity is desirable at a given point in time.

LINOWES: I suggest we may be getting off the track here if we try to attack too much of the problem at a symposium such as this. The facets of the subject are almost limitless.

I noticed recently that the forthcoming international Stockholm Conference on The Environment has found its work extending to cover pollution of outer space. I throw that in as an indication of the possibilities for expanding into almost limitless problem areas.

TANNENBAUM: But note too the current haggling between the West Germans and the East Germans and the announced intention of the Soviet Bloc to boycott the conference. Political ploys always get in the way of efforts like this, and it would be well to give them due consideration ahead of time.

DAVIDSON: Dave Linowes?

LINOWES: I would like to bring us back to the primary thrust of this symposium and suggest three areas for consideration—first, micro socioeconomic measurements: what is a company doing about pollution and other social needs? These measurements are possible; all they require is application. Second, macro socioeconomic measurements. These take in the whole economy. They include questions about performance by entire industries—therefore some level of organization larger than the corporation, such as the federal government, has to deal with macro problems. Third, there are the questions having to do with nonprofit institutions—schools, prisons, welfare agencies, and so on. As I see it, these are the levels at which problems exist, and I'd like to see us work around all three of them.

May I say further that I believe it is critical that persons in different disciplines change their state of mind. The attitude today is that we operate in our own little cubicles. We have to learn that accountants can benefit from social scientists, that social scientists can benefit from accountants and business executives. Each of us can contribute; the difficulty is one of communication.

As for the measurements we use, I don't think we have to wait for norms, any more than we have to wait for standard costs in a business to maintain effective controls. We maintain controls through comparisons. This same principle of comparisons which is used in everyday accounting practice can be used in our social efforts.

MARLIN: That is the approach we've taken at the Council.

LINOWES: To complete my comments, may I urge that in these deliberations we do not try to take on too much, that we recognize that a great deal can be accomplished now by the members of the various disciplines represented here.

TUNSTALL: From among the three areas you've mentioned, I'd like to see concentration on the corporation. I think the private sector can move very rapidly in the area of social reporting because a great deal of information is already on hand or readily available. There are three areas in which all major institutions, including corporations, can and should report to the public. They should tell us about the working conditions of employees, the process of production, and the use of the product.

Let's begin with the employee and working conditions. There may be as many as 10 to 15 different aspects of employee benefits and working conditions that, to some extent, companies report about to government now. But, of course, that information is not published by the government firm-by-firm. It is published in statistical tables only and no one knows about individual firms. Individual firms could tell us about salaries and wages; promotion rates by grade of employees; minority hiring and promotion; injury rates and other occupational hazards; transportation to work, by mode and time and cost; recreation facilities; child care; health and life insurance; retraining programs; sabbatical leaves; retirement, and so on. And I don't mean in the form of a fancy brochure—I mean in a comprehensive framework that will communicate this information to the public. This approach would make possible the measurement by comparison that has been talked about here.

The second area of reporting is the production process: to what extent does the production of a product pollute the environment, disrupt or change transportation systems, place new need for services on government, and so on?

The third area is the use of the product. How is the product used? With what results? What hazards to the consumer and what benefits? All major corporations should begin to report this information to the public and CPAs can participate by making sure these reports are accurate.

DAVIDSON: Al, I'd like to ask you what you think are the most important problems to attack?

BIDERMAN: As you have gone around the room, my ideas of the most important problems have changed after each speaker has told us his. I guess the first feeling I get from this discussion is that there might be a good deal of profit in thinking about many of the developments under discussion as responses of some broad social movements that might be regarded, in effect, as attacks on Milton Friedman, particularly the view of the centrality of the market system as a generator of measurements of goods and bads.

What happens to a social movement, any kind of social movement, right off, is that those who feel threatened try to neutralize it by partially incorporating the appeals of the movement. This kind of response has been true of the movement for more and better measurement—like the attempts to change the GNP to reflect nonmarketed services or to develop tax incentives that will help "internalize externalities" such as pollution, and other ways of assimilating criticisms of conventional economic thought and the economic arrangements derived from it in such ways as to involve the least change in both.

Not all the failings to which the social indicators movement is a response can be assimilated easily—these are problems in which everything is "externalities." These are problems of information, of where preference distributions come from, and so on, which cannot be grasped within economics nor handled by markets. I am very much in favor of the results of this partial incorporation, but one of the things I think we should avoid is the total equating of social and economic measurement. There are some thrusts in this movement that are not captured by incorporation into economic theory or market-based institutions.

With specific regard to the matter of measurements, I think lots of what is involved is essentially the inability of systems to attach value measures to matters of collective choice, to handle those things that are not properly registerable in terms of benefits to specific individuals. With regard to pollution, for example, there is no conceivable way to disaggregate the distribution of goods that are consumed collectively.

From the standpoint of values, one of the most important misunderstandings involved in these instances of measurement is the search for "output measures" in the social area. I think most of what we agree upon as "social" are things that cannot be assimilated in the market system. When looking for social output measures, we are looking for something we don't insist on for marketable goods and services—that is, an ultimate test of intrinsic value. In looking at the market as a measure of value, we accept the judgment of buyers that whatever is chosen was worth choosing at the price. We don't attempt to mastermind him, to decide whether he really got what he bargained for, that it really made him better off. I think we should look much more often for an equivalent kind of measure of choices in the public goods area, if we are going to stay with economic thinking. What we are working on are systems of presenting evidence regarding particular choices for particular ends that are persuasive enough to convince whomever has to be convinced to make an outlay of scarce resources to that end.

The whole public would have to be convinced of the importance of something before there could be some ultimate measures sought by this movement. For any input measure we use, agents of the public of various kinds would have to be convinced to buy something. So we are talking about organized systems of accountability for the allocation of scarce goods and resources for public purposes. This cannot be a matter of how much one particular individual or set of individuals gains. It seems very useful to me to present aggregate indicators of the distributions of the choices we make through collective and communal agencies of decision.

The second thing I think is important is to move our thoughts from the prescriptive, which I think our discussion tends to be exclusively, to the descriptive. What is going on? Who is doing what in social measurement—and why? Some projects along that line are already being undertaken, efforts to outline the distribution of activities in what is now an enormous industry—that devoted to evaluation of social programs and measuring social conditions and change.

I am myself engaged in a study to evaluate for the government the performance of contract firms—largely commercial firms—offering to perform evaluation studies in certain areas of social concern. In HEW and the Labor Department lists for 35 such evaluation studies on which they'd requested proposals, we identified more than 1,400 firms and nonprofit organizations as interested enough in this kind of business to want copies of the request for proposals (RFP) on one or more of these subjects. Then we are also beginning a study to determine what social science work goes on outside the academic sector; and the list of organizations we have identified so far shows that a great diversity of organizations—accounting firms, law firms, system analysis, aerospace companies—are tending to undertake social measurement.

DAVIDSON: Ian, we come to you.

WILSON: I am going to submit four ideas dealing with (1) change in the structure of corporate decision-making and goal-setting; (2) change in the internal management measurement system; (3) disclosure of corporate information; and (4) the need to start somewhere on social reporting. In 10 years we may be embarrassed by the simplicity of our beginning efforts at reporting on corporate "social action," but we've simply got to make a start—and soon.

It seems to me that the nature of corporate social performance has three aspects: first, making contributions to the attainment of national goals; second, conducting corporate operations in a socially responsible manner; third, getting outside one's walls, outside one's immediate sphere of business activity, either alone or in consortiums or in cooperation with government, and getting involved in problems of local communities where one has important operations.

With respect to contributing to national goals, it is necessary that long-term political and social factors be taken into account in the corporation's setting of its own goals. I would like to suggest that the most socially responsible thing General Electric can do in the next decade is not so much in the second area of performing operations in a socially responsible way—such as meeting pollution control standards or hiring minority groups or promoting women—as in moving, in a more systematic and concerted way, into such areas as health care, waste management, and transportation systems.

I was interested in the several remarks this morning about the need for measurements that are predictive of social change and of social expectations and desires. There are market opportunities in these changes as well as constraints with which a company must deal. I think that all these factors, which together make up the nature of the social performance of corporations, need to be made clear at the very beginning. And these factors must be considered, not as peripheral matters, but as integral elements in a company's strategic planning and long-range decision-making.

My point about changing the internal management measurement systems rests on the fact that merely making policy statements that establish corporate policies with respect to goals in particular social areas will be largely ineffective if you do not, at the same time, build some order of definite and regular measurement of internal management performance. You have to require that managers, each in his particular area of responsibility, gear into their operations some goals in the areas of corporate policy such as pollution control, equal employment opportunities, product safety, and so on. Then managers' performance must be measured and evaluated periodically against the goals that were set and agreed on with their superiors.

The third point I wanted to make is that business has got to bite the bullet on disclosure of corporate information. This is an area perhaps where the accounting fraternity can stand us in good stead. The tendency is always to panic at disclosing information and to say this is confidential and proprietary. "Bull" is the appropriate answer to that—in many cases. I don't know exactly where the limits lie, we have to establish what they should be. Perhaps there is safety, or comfort, in numbers here; perhaps we can develop some guidelines for disclosure on a joint basis rather than company-by-company.

*At 4 o'clock Thursday afternoon all participants reassembled, and* PROF. BROOKS, *for the group that had met with* PROF. CHURCHILL, *and* MR. BUTCHER, *for the group that had met with* DEAN DAVIDSON, *gave brief reports of the separate discussions. Following their summaries, there was general discussion as follows.*

SCARLOTT: Perhaps it would be helpful if I outlined for the group as a whole the point I was trying to make in the smaller group. What I was expressing was, partly, concern for the excitement that can surround popular issues and that can lead to ill-advised courses. A goal of zero pollution, for example, is a fairly demonstrable case of a norm that will draw upon resources beyond justification. I don't personally—nor does my organization—reject the idea of society's establishing norms based on the best available information, including inputs from the affected organizations as to what the cost alternatives are and what their ideas are of a socially acceptable standard. There is no argument at all if society decides what it wants out of business in these matters, realizes what the costs are, is willing to meet those costs in the form of the necessary prices, and makes that clear. But where I think business would be less than responsible is in going very far beyond the consensus of society, deciding on some very costly standards by itself, and then using its resources to get there. I see that as a way to waste resources on a massive scale. Work on urban problems has often led to counter-productive results by different organizations taking different tacks.

In saying those things I don't think I'm being negative about business responsibility. What I hope we don't do in pursuing these new social ends is to lose sight of business' responsibility to utilize resources efficiently. I think that is a valuable social end in itself. We ought to retain that while seeking better understanding of how to achieve additional social ends through the process of better measurement of the costs and the benefits.

MARLIN: You mentioned zero pollution whereas a more realistic figure might be control of 90 to 95 percent of emissions.

SCARLOTT: Yes, there is a vast difference between zero pollution and 90 percent control, or whatever is available with present technology. In the present state of the art, business needs to improve the quality of the input, and share more of its knowledge as to what the costs are. A problem is that if we talk about the costs, the estimates can be used against us, sometimes selectively and unfairly.

DAVIDSON: Al Biderman made several good points. One of them is that we tend to get hung up on the *normative* uses of any sort of measurement. We should keep in mind that *descriptive* measurements can be useful—even if we're not sure at the outset how they are going to be used. They can be valuable simply because they build a general body of knowledge.

The other point which I think well taken is that there is much more going on in social measurement right now than what we are aware of individually. More effort is needed to chart what is going on at the present time.

BAUER: Another good point of Al's was his comparison of social measurement with phenomena in the marketplace. In the latter case, a criterion of measurement is what people will pay for things—consumers' choices, an aggregation of many individuals' and groups' judgments of worth. Obviously many of these judgments are highly subjective. I think this suggests a research proposition in which you'd study how the judgmental process would affect the uses of social measurements. For example, a corporate social audit would generally have two types of judges making decisions about it. One is the external public, and the other is the corporation's management. You might do a study by confronting representatives of these two groups with simulated data at successively different levels of assumption. Research like this might give us some guide as to types of measures we ought to aspire to and the ways in which we could display them.

TUNSTALL: There has been interest among the public and the government in setting up an institute or some such group to help advise the government about the information it collects in the social areas—the kind of information I was talking about this morning. It looks as if the National Science Foundation is willing to help set up such an institute which would have its own board of directors drawn from both the private and public sectors. The reason I mention it is that the sooner something like this is set up, the more help an organization like the American Institute of Certified Public Accountants can get in this area. An institute of this nature would publish a newsletter, communicate research findings, develop a library, hold conferences, and possibly sponsor research. Something like this is in the works. How it will develop depends largely upon the people who are in this room.

MARLIN: In the relationship between profit and social action, which comes first?

MR. SAVOIE: Some people say you have to make a lot of money to be socially responsible. That sounds pretty cynical, but perhaps what is meant is that you have to have a lot of money to take social action that's broadly effective.

WILSON: A company that refuses to move—to respond to social demands until compelled to do so—is almost certainly restricting its freedom of action and increasing its eventual costs.

McComb: It is sometimes suggested that a sense of social responsibility is an indication of the quality of management. A management that is alert to its social responsibility would also be alert to other trends, and this would give them the ability to earn a greater profit than firms which didn't take the broad view.

Davidson: That's an interesting hypothesis. I have to point out, however, that Boise Cascade recently wrote off a substantial sum that was largely related to a venture involving social responsibility.

Scarlott: I've talked about business' social actions starting out in its own backyard. If a company isn't an equal opportunity employer, I don't think it can offset that by good marks for its charitable contributions. Clearly it's in the interests of society and of an individual business as well for that business to understand the direction of society and to travel in that direction itself. Means are available to business for getting a reasonably reliable indication of changes that are occurring and from which further changes can be extrapolated. I believe that if social measurement better captures the character of society, the changes in it, and the directions of it, business is intelligent enough to respond by accommodating to those trends. Maybe not all of business, but most of it. This would surely be one of the large benefits from improved measurement. I don't want to say this could be taken for granted, but I would bet that business is sharp enough to see handwriting on the wall.

Wilson: I take it as not inconsistent with the measurement of corporate social performance to consider our highly developed production and distribution system as having not only economic value but social value. It seems to me legitimate to say that business in an earlier day was socially responsible just by creating jobs, or by contributing to the material standard of living, which were predominant social goals at that time. If society's wants are changing, if more is wanted beyond basic necessities, is it not legitimate to say that there is a measure of corporate responsibility in its performance in attending to these later needs?

CHURCHILL: Perhaps there has been too much emphasis on the negative side of industrial production. What *is* the social report of a business? Do I eliminate the social values the marketplace puts upon the firm's products? They are wanted; therefore they fill a social need. How do I distinguish between production of protein and of air conditioners? Do I look at the things in the social area which the economic measures don't capture? Do I supplement the economic measures by the contributions to pollution control—to employment? The question troubles me, which is why I raise it.

WILSON: I have no argument with supplementing the economic measures with what David Linowes terms socioeconomic accounting. I *do* object to saying that the economic area gives no indication of corporate social performance.

LINOWES: You're right. Industry is doing many things that contribute to the solution of what are today termed social problems. Research on pollution-control devices is an example. Business organizations take on contracts dealing with such things as education of the disadvantaged. There are projects for taking over garbage and trash collection. On the international level, developing nations such as Iran and Greece engage American companies to help them with big jobs. These engagements are undertaken with the idea of making a profit, of course. But I think there should be a clear recognition that profit-making is not necessarily incompatible with social progress.

TOAN: Despite adverse comment you hear, not all people outside of business disparage profits; they tend to look on them as something very legitimate and desirable.

EISNER: I don't believe the issue is between economic indicators and social indicators. The question is really a matter of finding an economic measure for many things that concern the quality of life. The important issue is how should business firms, in their accounting, handle expenditures that are presumably in the broad public interest—expenditures, for instance, to diversify the labor force, or to improve Detroit, or whatever it might be. There might be an effort to estimate how much of the expenditure is designed to increase the capital value of the firm, and how much to achieve something outside of the interests of the firm. My own guess—it's almost an article of faith—is that almost all expenditures are aimed at improving the prospects for the firm's capital value. They may spend a good bit trying to prevent legislation which would tend to lessen the value of the firm, too. I feel this is the basis for having not only an enlightened accounting but for having firms concentrate on making profits and at the same time having the broad society concentrate on seeing to it that social needs are met.

I don't like to see us getting involved in questions of the direction of society when we should be first concerned with the matter of accounting itself. I would agree that it is necessary to understand the tremendous amount that business firms already do. But I would take considerable exception to any notion that you can depend upon private firms, seeking profits, to do things that are not in the interest of the firm but are useful to society. If industry is competitive, its operations are inevitably in the interests of society.

I think what has brought us together are matters the market system cannot meet, and these are matters that revolve around questions of externalities—questions of social costs which it is not in the interest of the business firm to meet. I think we delude ourselves if we think the remedy is for companies to do things which it is not in their interest to do.

TOAN: Is it true that these activities are ignored in most statistics?

EISNER: The statistics almost consistently ignore them—with one exception—and that is the depreciation of capital. Yet the calculation of depreciation is where I think the accountants have failed miserably—largely because of the tax authorities. You have all sorts of arbitrary rules that are made all the more arbitrary because of tax considerations. For the most part we stick to cases of market transactions, and obviously these do not measure a huge element in the quality of life. Take family life—when we talk about surveying human happiness, I suppose the biggest single thing is the state of life in the family. But it is not a market transaction and so we don't measure it.

DAVIDSON: As I have listened to the discussion this morning and afternoon, I have been struck by how much of the conversation about social measurement has focused on corporate enterprise. But the mix of organizations in American society has changed. The public sector now comprises a larger part of the whole. But I've heard only one person talk about social measurement, and about the aim of improving the quality of life, in connection with the biggest industry in the U.S.—education. I see more resistance to social measurement in the universities and the public school system than I see in business.

BIDERMAN: But it's also the social area in which quantitative measurement has been longest practiced. Toan spoke this morning about accountants doing more of this than anyone else, but think of schoolteachers . . . they grade papers, compute ratios, do all that aptitude testing. And there are so many more teachers than there are accountants.

*Start of Friday Session*

CHURCHILL: Yesterday we talked about a great many subjects . . . covered a great deal of territory. Today we'd like to get down more to specifics, and we felt a way of doing this would be with some case studies. I have asked Bernie to outline some of the social areas his bank is trying to work on—what have they accomplished, where have they been hung up, what data they need. Perhaps this will evoke some suggestions, criticism, elucidations, and so on.

BUTCHER: I welcome this assignment as an opportunity to get some free consulting service. Since I have only recently picked up the social audit project, let me say first that the thrust of my remarks will reflect my own views only and not necessarily those of my employer.

I want to start off with a little historical background. You may recall that the Bank of America has been the target of several incidents of social protest—as when our Isla Vista branch was burned in 1970. I don't want you to think that's the primary reason we are doing what we are doing, but during that period some of our people began thinking that the social action question called for further attention.

A high-level committee was appointed and charged with establishing some priorities—to consider the social programs a private institution such as ours could engage in. The purpose was a) to filter out those areas of concern not within the bank's realm and b) to concentrate on the achievable.

The committee identified four main areas where the bank could make a contribution in California—minorities, housing, the environment, and an amorphous area labeled social unrest. Next an inventory was taken of what the bank was already doing in those areas. The result was this booklet [*Mr. Butcher displays it*] which lists our activities in each of the priority areas. Some of the items are quite small and some quite significant. No attempt was made to weight one program against another or to evaluate overall impact.

I did not have my present job at the time and did not take part in preparing the list; but when I saw it, I was chiefly interested in the criteria used in its preparation. The list seems to be composed of programs undertaken for reasons other than, or in addition to, the normal profit-maximization motive. Although the list includes many programs that bring a profit, that profit is generally less than it would have been had the funds been invested in other areas.

Meanwhile, our president was concerning himself in this matter of social measurement. He is a relatively young man with 20 years or so until normal retirement. I would guess that as he looks ahead he feels his term of service will be judged heavily on the basis of the bank's response to changing social demands.

In some public statements he urged the development of what he called "the arithmetic of quality," both on a national scale and adapted to private enterprise. He did not specifically outline the "arithmetic of quality"—he was merely calling on people like you in this room to begin thinking in these terms.

President Clausen then issued a charge to our Controller's Department to look at our list of social activities to see if some overall measurement could be made of the cost and effectiveness of our efforts. Incidentally, the question of where in a corporation responsibility for such an assignment ought to lie may be something we will want to discuss. A controller may be a bit nonplussed, because his major concern has traditionally been expense control, dollar figures, and the bottom line.

Anyway, an effort was then made to assign costs to the items in the inventory—the cost for each item during the previous year, the cumulative costs for each item, and an estimate of what the costs will be in the future. Most of these cost calculations were extremely rough and based on a large number of assumptions—but they have given us a good starting point for rationally evaluating our social programs.

The social audit project has now been picked up by my boss, Mr. G. Robert Truex, who has recently been appointed Executive Vice President in charge of Social Policy. We would like to build on the base of what has been done in the bank so far—to get something down on paper and let people shoot at it. Even a crude first effort will contribute to the "state of the art" of social accounting and help management in the evaluation of its socially oriented objectives.

The format of such a report should allow management to relate the costs of its social programs to the long-range benefits to the company. Factored into this calculation should be an estimate of the benefits accruing to society from our programs. A report of this type should help management see where a particular program might be revised to make it more effective. It should also establish a model against which various proposed new programs can be checked to assure that they are well thought out and effective in practice.

Our approach to the social audit has, to date, been a horizontal one—a program by program, cost vs. benefit approach. This contrasts with the vertical tack being taken by Chase Manhattan in New York.

Chase has isolated a few geographical areas in New York where they have branches serving a homogeneous but stagnant area and have determined to aim the bulk of their normal activities and special programs toward these areas.

They intend to channel their aid to education, housing, minority business loans, and so on, into these geographical areas, with the expectation that the several programs will reinforce one another and improve the general prospects in the area. The results would be measurable in the growth of business at the branch. In addition, they have developed a four-page list of macro indicators which they feel will reflect the effects of their programs on the defined areas of New York in which they are operating.

I personally think this approach suffers from all the problems associated with macro indicators that we discussed yesterday. How good are the indicators? How should they be weighted? What part of the demonstrated change can one institution attribute to its own limited input? How do you evaluate which programs are effective and which are not?

The second approach, which I think is preferable, is the horizontal. Under this approach, each program is evaluated on the basis of its costs and its benefits, both to the company and to the general business community. As a beginning, we could take a limited number of items appearing on our inventory of social activities—starting with those that seem most amenable to measurement—and concentrate on them. Examples might be our special home-loan program, which channels mortgage funds at reduced rates and reduced qualifications to minorities; the SBA business loan program for minorities, or the government-guaranteed student loan program, of which we are a major underwriter in California.

Let me take our student loan program and follow through this type of horizontal analysis, using some hypothetical numbers. Assume that the Bank of America in 1972 will make 10,000 student loans. We would first analyze the costs associated with making these 10,000 loans. One element of this cost would, of course, be the difference in interest received on student loans as compared with that which could have been realized by channeling the funds in normal ways. This would, of course, depend heavily on an assumption of the level of demand for ordinary consumer credit. A countervailing cost element would be the low risk on student loans since they are government-guaranteed. Higher administration costs and delinquency ratios would also have to be factored in. For purposes of discussion, let us say these costs add up to about $250,000 a year.

Once costs are pinned down to a reasonable extent, the elements of benefit should be isolated. We start off by listing those *long-range* benefits the bank might expect to receive over a ten-year period. Discounting this return to present value would give a meaningful comparison to annual costs. (Ten years actually mean six years of payback, since the first repayments are not made until four years after the loan is made.)

The first element of benefit is the profit the bank expects from new customers developed by the student loan program. Now, since our share of the banking business in California is about 30 percent, we might expect to get 30 percent of those 10,000 young people as customers in any event. But if 5,000 became customers after graduation, there is an increment of 2,000 customers, the profits from which could reasonably be attributed to the student loan program. Average annual profit is $40 per customer, so an increment of 2,000 customers can be computed as an $80,000 addition to profit annually.

The second element of long-range benefit that might be attributable to the student loan program would be any increase in the level of income of the students who would theoretically have become our customers anyway, but who wouldn't have gone to college without a loan. The profit differential between a high-school-graduate customer and a college-graduate customer between the ages of 25 and 35 is, say, $15 a year. The higher profit on a college-graduate customer results both from his higher income and the fact that he does more banking business. We must be careful to include only those customers enabled to go to college by student loans.

The third benefit to the bank that one can hypothesize is much more conjectural. It is the indirect profit from those other 5,000 who don't bank with us afterward—the increment to the state economy caused by those who wouldn't otherwise have gone to college. If they make an additional $5,000 a year, the benefit to the state economy is $25 million, and the share of this to the Bank of America. . . [*Mr. Butcher joins in general laughter.*]

However horseback the figures are, this approach can lead to a lot of rethinking of existing programs. For example, to reduce our losses on the student loan program—to cut down on those who had been giving us problems—we established a requirement that, in order to get a loan, the student had to have had an account with us for at least six months.

But consider—if the student has had an account with us for six months, he's most likely going to continue being a customer, so the benefit to the bank in terms of incremental customer gain from the program goes way down. The requirement might also tend to reduce the number of loans to minority groups. So, this type of social audit might reveal that we are not only adversely affecting the long-term benefits to the bank from an economic standpoint but are also adversely affecting the social objectives we hoped to achieve.

Or suppose a quick review of the difficulties associated with student loans reveals that most problems come from freshmen—so we discontinue granting loans to freshmen. Well, if a student can pay his way through the first year of college, the odds are probably that he can pay for his total education. So the benefit of the program to the bank in terms of the higher incomes earned by college graduates goes way down because these people would have gone to college anyway.

It seems to me that an audit structure such as this could develop into a valuable management tool. It could help to formalize program objectives and to isolate the variables that can be manipulated to improve performance and increase return.

Another result of this type of audit format might be a change in the way managements view social programs. The traditional view is that these programs are basically philanthropic—a controllable expense to be minimized but not necessarily monitored for effectiveness. By calling for an ongoing cost-benefit type of analysis, we might be able to move these programs from the philanthropic mode to the normal investment mode common to mainstream business thinking.

Returning to the student loan example, our analysis might reveal that the *net* cost of the program is closer to $50,000 a year than the previously calculated $250,000. The final question, then, is: are the social effects we are trying to achieve worth $50,000?

The answer to this question is largely subjective, but the first step is to clearly list the social objectives of the program in question. I know of very few corporate social programs that are entered into because somebody set out all the objectives and thought about all the possible consequences. Just to sit down and write out the objectives for a program is a step in the right direction. Such things as improved self-development opportunities, development of better communities, and improved knowledge of consumer credit might be mentioned as social objectives of the student loan program.

The degree to which these social objectives are met cannot be determined in precise dollar terms. But periodic surveys and interviews with the recipients of our student loans—as well as with our own people—can go a long way toward monitoring the impact of our program on the larger society. This information would give us a better feel for whether or not our $50,000 "societal investment" was actually paying off.

BAUER: I want to thank Bernie for that presentation. It has given me some ideas for ways to analyze the objectives and benefits of programs I hadn't thought about, and possibly to improve them.

BUTCHER: Does that mean I get a raise?

[*Voice*]: If you do, that will affect the cost-benefit ratio. [*Laughter*]

BIDERMAN: Bernie's presentation raises the interesting question of how, from a political point of view, you handle social activities. Traditionally, in this country and other countries, higher education has been publicly financed as a social good, rather than exclusively a private one. If business organizations did not support efforts of a political administration which has other ideas of the proper level of the costs and benefits of education to society, political forces would be that much bigger a factor to take into computation. Through the political process, there might emerge an entirely different approach than you are taking. Bernie's emphasis is on costs and benefits to individual persons and corporations as opposed to the assumption that higher education brings benefits to society as a whole rather than just to the individual. I see the bank as involved in the political process. If banks were reluctant to make loans, political forces would be applied to twist their arms.

EISNER: In computing opportunity costs, you would not want to overlook some other comparisons—for example, the social benefits that would result if money were not used for student loans but for aid to business or other purposes. The position of the Bank of America in its community—the state of California—is unique in that it has such a major role in the California economy. Also there's the fact that students are not as likely to leave the state, as they are elsewhere. In an area where certain firms are predominant, they can and often do function as a form of government.

Now for most firms around the country, the conditions in which Bank of America operates do not prevail. When a company becomes so large an element in the community, it *has* to take action in social areas or it's going to be in for all sorts of trouble—a target of much criticism, possibly adverse legislation. I don't know if Bank of America's approach to these problems is the right one, but surely it's good public relations. If it cost $50,000 or $100,000, in PR terms it may be worth millions.

ALBERS: As Bernie has said, it's much easier to figure costs than benefits. He mentioned lack of study of the benefits. It would be desirable for the judgments to come from the public's side rather than the corporation's. With the public's point of view in mind we can weigh the costs against the social and corporate benefits.

McCOMB: Another reason it's desirable to have society place the value on these activities is that business might tend to overstate it, to get too enthusiastic. It would be better for some outside agency to come up with the value against which business could measure its contribution.

TOAN: If the evaluation could separate internal and external benefits, it could be helpful to a company management when it had to choose between two programs. One would, in fact, suspect that if one could get the best compromise between the internal and external benefits, one would in the long run produce the greatest aggregate benefit. A company might put a lot of effort into something that had very little public impact, whereas if it somewhat reduced its internal benefits, it might in total produce something of considerably greater value.

I did not gather from your presentation, Bernie, that any of your findings or projections resulted from an interdisciplinary study. I think it is very important, as I've said before, that neither accountants nor sociologists nor psychologists should feel that they are the ones who can give all or even necessarily the right answers on their own. Does the Bank of America contemplate that its planning and subsequent measurement of social programs will involve interdisciplinary effort?

BUTCHER: If I thought the information that could be gathered by a joint effort would be more useful, I'd be in favor of it.

*Second Half of Friday Session*

CHURCHILL: The other person I've asked to present a case is Stu McElyea.

McELYEA: I imagine that even before Bernie spoke, all of you knew what The Bank of America is. But I doubt that many of you have as good an idea of the General Accounting Office. We are a group of more than 4,500 people in the legislative branch of the federal establishment, headed by the Controller General of the United States. To put it simply, we can be described as the independent auditors in the federal establishment.

We have a number of roles given to us by statute, but I think that for purposes of this discussion the roles that are pertinent are those of *accountant* and *auditor*. Mainly, these functions are intended to respond to the needs of Congress for information about the many programs which are underway and are managed by the Executive branch.

Perhaps a rather simplistic description of what Congress does in this respect would help you understand where we fit in. In a great number of actions every year, the Congress decides how much of the national resource is going to be devoted to federal programs, and engages in the process of allocating funds among them. Congress is continually concerned about how well the managers in the Executive branch did with what they were given last year. And that's where we in GAO spend most of our time—looking to see what happened to $200 billion plus.

We often wish that we could stay in the traditional role of auditors and look at measurements which executive managers themselves make of their activities, but most often we are being asked to accept what they do as a matter of faith. As I said yesterday, we experience a great deal of frustration in trying to respond to requests of Congress for information and not finding any definitive set of standards in existence for the programs we're looking at. As a consequence, one of the things we're beginning to do is to suggest to the Congress that they, as the financing body, ought to insist that the executives say what it is they're intending to do, and develop standards as a baseline for a determination.

Neil has suggested that some specific examples might help you to understand what it is we're about. One that I recall from recent years is our study of the attempts to reduce pollution in a New England river basin. We found that, because of lack of planning, a great deal of work had been done with little effect. Grants were given to communities which were interested in having the funds but there was no plan for the river basin as a whole. So Town A cleaned up its discharges into the river, which was immediately repolluted by Town B just below. The net effect on the river was zero.

I think I mentioned yesterday our having been involved in one of the Aid to Families with Dependent Children programs; it was called WIN, the acronym for Work Incentive. We found in Denver and in Los Angeles that it had in fact resulted in removing some people from the relief rolls. Another thing we found, though, was that the program, as designed in the legislation, contained a disincentive for the male members of these families. The result of having trained these males to the point where they could obtain employment at, say, $250 a month caused them to lose payments from the government of maybe $300 monthly. So the net cost to the family of becoming a working member of society was $50 a month. We have reported on this to the Congress, and it is now being considered there.

Something I hope we are going to become engaged in is a review of the Colorado River Storage project. Here is a report by the Bureau of Reclamation on that project during 1971. The project stretches from up in Wyoming—the Green River—almost to Arizona—the Hoover Dam. The report is particularly interesting to me because it is one of the first I have seen that attempts to deal with more than just the project activities themselves. There is an investment here of about $900 million, and the report this year includes not only the financial results of the generation and sale of power, the impoundment and use of water for irrigation, and so on, but also a section about environmental activities. It reports on the recreational benefits; on fishing activity; and although the report does not do so itself, there have been some economic figures attached to it: the fish caught in one of its projects are worth so much, the recreation days in one of the areas are worth so much.

Whether the numbers are good, I don't know. But if we undertake it this year, it will be a first attempt by us to state an opinion about an agency report that contains something more than just financial statements. I am already convinced that one of the things that will be said about it is that it has some notable omissions. For example, it says nothing about the salinity problem in the lower Colorado River. The water is almost as salty as the Pacific Ocean as a result of irrigation. A good percentage of the water that is used on the farms runs back into the river, and it leaches salt out of the soil and into the river.

I recall also having made a review of the student loan program that we have talked about here. I regret that I don't remember very much about it, but I do recall that we noted the high delinquency rate with some alarm.

Our organization engages in 150 to 200 of these examinations every year, many of them in the defense area. It may be, as Al Biderman said yesterday, that there's a great deal underway in measuring the performance of social managers. From our point of view I must say that it is very well concealed. Over the past five years particularly, we have made great effort to find these measures, and we have had little success. Perhaps the reason is that what we're looking for is not what Al considers social measures.

What we need, simply stated, is a determination, by the managers themselves, of how well their programs are accomplishing whatever their purposes may be. And we need this program-by-program, not in the aggregate once a year or once every five years, because the Congress considers programs every year, either to provide additional resources or withhold them. I agree with Art Naftalin that a great many of these decisions are not made on the basis of numbers provided by accountants. They're political. But it is our view that the Congress ought to have the best information that we can give them.

I would agree also with the comment made yesterday that what we need to do is get started. Perhaps we could launch, as I believe Justin was saying yesterday, an experimental study of educational results; maybe we ought to look around at Bernie here and at what is going on at The Bank of America. And I surely would like to see included at least one study in the governmental area. Whether or not these are the best suggestions as to the way to proceed, it seems to me that the one thing we do not have is the luxury of time to spare.

I may be wrong, but I think I detect growing disenchantment in the Congress with programs they are asked to accept on faith. These programs are massive—the costs are enormous—and I'd like to repeat again my suggestion of yesterday that whether we involve these costs in the national income accounts, or whether we do it as a matter of cost/benefit analysis, or whether we do it in a way that is closer to what Art Toan and I understand accounting to be, we have to get a higher degree of rationality into the determination of what are the costs and what are the benefits. We accountants, I believe, have always insisted that a particularly useful approach is to develop information that can be compared to something.

BUTCHER: Is the report you mentioned—the one by the Bureau of Reclamation—an example?

McELYEA: Well, I'll grant you, it's a very mild beginning. But it does make some attempt to relate activities to results. There are things that are not in it—nothing about flood control, for instance. What we are urging is that agencies which engage in activities begin to account for these activities in all the ways that they used to justify the creation of the project at the outset. The unfortunate thing is that this Bureau of Reclamation report didn't raise much of a ripple; it is one of the very few attempts by the Bureau to enlarge the scope of its reporting and it cost money. And not having got much attention, it may be abandoned.

MR. ANDERSON: Among the many programs you examine, I assume there are some in the antipoverty area. Perhaps this may offer grounds for a small experiment. You have X Community, the proper population size, a definite poverty problem, and a program instituted. Would this not provide the basis for an experiment in social measurement to determine the effectiveness of such a program over a period of time?

McELYEA: It certainly would, David. The WIN program I mentioned was implemented in the city and county of Los Angeles at about the same time the aerospace industry was in substantial decline. Nothing you could do probably would have reduced the rate of unemployment. Because of decline in the whole local economy, unemployment was increasing so fast that it was very hard to tell what the effect of this program was on the community.

We are now trying to work out a method in Arizona for looking at all the things the federal establishment is doing for an Indian tribe and see if we can tell what is happening in consequence. This is different from looking in one instance at what we're trying to do for the tribe in the matter of housing, in another instance at the educational programs, and at another time at medical programs or income maintenance. We're going to try to put it all together, and the Indian tribe we have in mind is fairly isolated so maybe we can tell something about the total. How you would do this for New York City, I just don't know.

BORUCH: There's a large-scale experiment being carried on by the Office of Economic Opportunity right now to determine how different levels of income maintenance affect the spending behavior, employment rate, and other characteristics of low-income and welfare groups.

McELYEA: You're speaking about New Jersey?

BORUCH: New Jersey, Oregon, Indiana, and Wisconsin. In New Jersey, OEO launched a big experiment involving the random assignment of people to different levels of income subsidy. Five or six thousand at least, I know, took part in New Jersey; comparisons among groups can then be made to determine, at the lowest level of ambiguity possible, which level of subsidy is "best" by some criterion. The process of randomization helps to ameliorate the problem of competing explanations of the efficacy of programs, something that a post hoc appraisal of a social indicator cannot hope to do.

McELYEA: It's not very attractive to deprive children for the purpose of comparing and telling how well the programs are working for those whose conditions are being improved.

BAUER: I'd like to hear more about the problems of experimentation here. I am more familiar with experimentation programs in a marketing context, and one of the things you find there is that the variation among localities is so large that in order to get a decent reading you have to have eight different locales in an experimental group, and eight different locales as controls. I've heard of few federal programs that were elaborate enough in design to allow for this.

CAMPBELL: I hear a lot about social experiments now, along with social indicators. These seem to be the two big things talked about.

And I think it's great that there is this enthusiasm. But I find that when we are approached by governmental agencies to undertake an assessment of some sort of program, almost always it is after the fact. Some program has been put into effect without any thought of assessment being built into it.

The alternatives for managing data are very restricted because the whole thing is already completed or its form fixed. Is Congress coming to believe that they'll be able to assess things better if some sort of feedback is designed into these programs at the beginning? Does GAO have any commitment to that philosophy, or are the political considerations that Bob talks about so overpowering that there is no possibility of establishing practical experimental situations?

McElyea: A few minutes ago I ascribed some opinions to Congress, and that was perhaps rash because it's obviously difficult to predict what Congress will or will not do. But I can speak for myself.

Certainly, I am sympathetic to your problem of being asked to evaluate a program after the fact and finding that nobody engaged in the operation has bothered to keep records about it, or, if records were kept, they don't really have much to do with assessment. But that's where we are and that's why I'm here. Because I'm convinced that somehow people who are undertaking these activities must develop, for their own purposes if not others', the kinds of criteria and measurements that will enable them to tell how well they're doing. As I said yesterday, I think that's the first need—for the managers to have it. It's unfortunate that we—or you—coming in after the fact, can't tell. But it's more serious that the managers of the work can't tell. I think that over a period of time, perhaps through competition for funding, those managers who do better in this matter of establishing standards for measuring what they hope to do, and then accounting for their activities by the same standards—that those managers will come to have an edge when they request funds. Maybe that's an idealistic hope and it won't happen. It would happen if I had anything to do with who will get the money.

Campbell: Is it part of the problem that the people who manage these programs haven't been able to conceptualize the kind of measurement that would be useful?

McELYEA: I don't think anybody has ever insisted on it, Angus. Justin, here, is from Cornell, and although I haven't been there, I'd wager that if you went to their accounting department or the business manager or controller, you won't find much that will tell you how well Cornell.is doing what it's up there to do. You'll find a balance sheet that will tell you what they own and owe, but that's not why they're there. They're very sophisticated at the receipts and disbursements kind of thing, and if Art Toan came up to make an audit, they'll say that everything's great. But what they'd be talking about is receipts and disbursements. As to how well they did in educating the students, and in research and the advance of knowledge—probably nothing. Yet all of us know that Cornell does a great job.

DAVIDSON: You're getting close to home now and you fight dirty.

[*Laughter*]

McELYEA: Not at all—I think we accountants are right in the midst of this and greatly at fault.

DAVIDSON: I do have some reservations about your proposal to have the people in programs make the evaluations of themselves. They've not been able to do it objectively in the past. I don't know whether they can do it. The level of prostitution in the evaluation process is high.

NAFTALIN: Who constitutes the proper agency for this kind of larger assessment or evaluation? The government has several possibilities. One is the route you've mentioned—to enlarge the accounting review to include assessment of the purposes of the legislation . . .

McELYEA: May I interpose a comment there? I do not believe that accountants should establish the standards for measuring the accomplishments of an educator or a sociologist or a doctor. What we're saying is that if these disciplines will do that, then we can help them account for the activity in terms of their own specialty.

NAFTALIN: This is an important restriction you're making.

McELYEA: I'm not at all interested in having accountants go around the country deciding what the standards ought to be for welfare programs or educational programs or medical programs. Accountants aren't equipped for that.

NAFTALIN: Then are you saying that accountants can provide the knowledge of accounts and procedures to fill in what the operating people feel are the proper criteria?

McELYEA: If you will go back to Minneapolis and run for and become Mayor again, I guarantee that if you call in the accountants and say: "I want a kind of accounting here in terms of what we are doing in our city—what can you do to help me begin to think about it," in such a case we can help you gather data, and we can analyze them and summarize them and help you understand them in ways that are pertinent to what you are doing.

NAFTALIN: You almost make me want to run for Mayor again.

[Laughter]

I think my concern about this question being resolved by GAO or similar agencies is that I conceive their orientation as being accounts and audits in the traditional sense. Don't misunderstand me—I don't say you couldn't do it, but I would be somewhat apprehensive about the relationship. I think that in the poverty program, or education, or law enforcement, or any of the other soft areas, I would raise the question: Why the General Accounting Office? I raise this question because I look upon the GAO as an organization that gives advice to Congress—post-audit advice with respect to programs that have been

completed. I would regard the operating agencies as more closely related to the ongoing pre-audit thing.

McElyea: That's part of my point.

Bauer: I guess no one would quarrel with the need to specify the
goals of a program, but from this conversation I get a feeling of a rigid
agreement, in advance, on things that will be audited. I think you will
agree that, in social programs, things happen that you hadn't anticipated when you started them, and that becomes extremely important when you make an evaluation downstream. Maybe we're smart
enough to build that in in advance. But going in after the fact, I think
one has to be flexible enough to discover that which hasn't been built
in but turns out to be important.

Oliphant: Ray, what you say is true, but the same thing holds with
a financial budget. There are unknowns which crop up during the
year and things do not come out as intended. But they can be ex-
plained and their importance assessed because at least there is a starting point. Performance can be measured against plans up to a point,
and then there are things that weren't foreseen—maybe couldn't have
been—when the plan was made. And explanatory comments and reasons are given. It seems to me there's a very direct analogy between
what you said and financial accounting.

Tunstall: Stu, if your group can look at only 150 to 200 projects a
year on behalf of Congress, and yet we know how many projects the
federal government is involved in and pays for, obviously the main
burden for evaluation and reporting of these lies with the Executive
branch.

McElyea: Which is where I think it belongs.

Tunstall: I don't think we have heard anything here that would indicate anything different. But I do want to raise the issue of the overall
direction of programs—is that better decided by the people running
them?

DAVIDSON: I'm not sure I agree. I agree that the managers of each specific program should have the responsibility for submitting their own evaluation of it. But you may not have adequate resources within the structure of the program to do this evaluation. You may need a structure, which may not be located within the program, to evaluate whether the program has been carried out in accordance with objectives.

McELYEA: May I say that our friends in the public sector of accounting are probably going to perform between 50,000 and 75,000 audits of some kind of federally financed activities this year. Most of those audits are purely financial at present. But it's likely that the only reservoir of talent around the country that can undertake the job of independent review is the public accountant.

BORUCH: The American Institute of Research just came out with a review of some 3,000 programs in education in primary and secondary schools. In their initial research proposal they said they'd do a cost/benefit analysis. I guess everybody suspected there'd be a big problem in establishing what the benefits were, but it turned out that the major problem—and the reason they couldn't do the analysis— was that they couldn't get any good, clear, standardized cost data on these 3,000 programs, all subsidized by the federal government. They got part of the necessary data, but didn't get much reliable, uniform information. Categories appear to have varied so much that it was virtually impossible to get a handle on the situation. Perhaps educators need better guidelines for documenting the costs of programs so that evaluators can do a better job in appraising the programs' effectiveness.

McELYEA: We call those principles of accounting.

BORUCH: And educators and social scientists aren't familiar enough with those.

OLIPHANT: That's why this group is here—to see if we can come up with some.

BAUER: I think I should communicate to this group that when I read some of their stuff, I get all "shook up" on the problem of evaluation because of the very complicated technical problems of design. Even though I am a social scientist, I don't feel that I really know this, and I suspect that some of the rest of you here are in the same fix. Take, for example, the Westinghouse evaluation of the Head Start project. There was a problem in matching up the kids who were in the program and those who were not—just a moderately sophisticated technical issue. But because it wasn't handled right, Westinghouse evaluated Head Start as producing nothing, and their finding probably was, at least in part, a consequence of the way the kids were matched.

I would hope that somehow the sort of stuff Don Campbell, and other people who are very sophisticated in the area of evaluation, have been writing up in the professional journals could be converted into more lay language, so that a group like this would begin to get some sense of these technical complications and of their great importance, and would also get some idea of whom to turn to when they find themselves in a situation of making program evaluations. They need technical assistance that I think they don't now even know they need.

BORUCH: That's one of the purposes of the Social Science Research Council committee on experimentation on planning evaluation of programs, not so much for academics as for the managers of programs. The objective here is to document the state of the art in large-scale randomized experiments for evaluating social programs. Social indicators will be discussed primarily as pointers to problems rather than solely as a device for actually helping to solve problems.

CAMPBELL: I doubt that that kind of expertise is ever going to be part of the common language.

BORUCH: I don't expect the expertise itself to be communicated but a realization of the importance of such expertise.

CAMPBELL: Quite so. It's like sampling. Ten or 20 years ago people were convinced you could draw samples just by stopping people on the street. By now, just about everybody is more sophisticated than that, but they still aren't sure how to draw samples.

TANNENBAUM: I suspect that the suggestion that the time has come for us to share knowledge is also a bit premature. Proper techniques for evaluation are not developed yet; we are just beginning to get a handle on them. Accordingly, we still have little to communicate to other people, in lay language or otherwise. We know what the problems are, but we haven't yet figured out ways of surmounting them.

BORUCH: The technical methods for evaluation in true experiments are well developed and highly articulated. It is the quasi-experiments which require research and the political-institutional techniques for implementing true experiments which are largely underdeveloped.

OLIPHANT: Should this be done in a compartmentalized way, or a little more broadly? I mean by psychologists working as one group, sociologists as another . . .

TANNENBAUM: There are a number of groups from the various disciplines working on various aspects of the matter. But who knows how long before these methods are far enough along? We have some procedures we can use now, but they're not foolproof. Even Don Campbell is having some second thoughts about some of the so-called quasi-experimental techniques he was proposing with great enthusiasm only a short while ago. We rightly have more confidence about controlled experiments, but the problems are in actual field situations, and I doubt our present-day society is prepared to accept some of the risks in running many needed true experiments.

BIDERMAN: As Stu mentioned, Congress is moving toward requiring that some of the money it spends on programs go to evaluation. Some programs are being organized explicitly for experimental purposes; the whole purpose of a program is the evaluation of social experiments. There are now vast expenditures—though not as vast as some would consider necessary—HEW is spending $30 million on evaluation. And that's just one department.

In the water resources area, legislation now requires that before you can even begin any major project the agency has to show not only the economic but also the social and environmental costs and benefits the program is designed to produce. There are elaborate guidelines as to what kind of data must be mustered—what kind of community discussions of the data. Throughout the country, these things are being done. They may be done stupidly, but at least some people have begun.

When you come to the role of the independent evaluation, the sort of thing GAO is getting involved in, I think perhaps that's where the resources might be used, that is, to be an independent evaluation of the evaluation activities undertaken by the executive arm or by independent evaluation study contractors it hires. This is essentially what goes on, anyway, in the financial audits. That is, the government auditor comes in and observes what the CPA of the activity has done. He does an audit of the audit. Perhaps, GAO's modest budget could go furthest if it sought to evaluate evaluations, rather than programs directly.

CHURCHILL: At this point perhaps we could use an audit of our own proceedings during the past day and a half. Justin?

DAVIDSON: Neil has asked me to try to put together a brief summary of our discussions. Let me apologize in advance for my defective hearing: I tend to hear only what I want to hear. With that caveat, I'll review some of the propositions that I've heard during the past two days. I have listed five major points.

A first point concerns our back-and-forth talk about social measurement and the social responsibility of organizations, particularly business organizations. We have two differing conceptual views of social responsibility, and these views affect how social measurement is approached. One view of the social responsibility of business is that it consists of maximizing profits within constraints set by society. The second view is that business should have multiple objectives—

profit *and* objectives that are "good" for society. I would emphasize that, in spite of these two differing views, I heard consensus. Whichever view one begins from, social measurement, in some form, is desirable.

A second point is that we must distinguish between the process of measuring and the process of attaching values or setting norms for what is measured. Distinguishing these two processes makes for clearer thinking. It serves to remind us that when we measure, we imply norms and values to some extent. A danger is always there: emphasizing particular values or implying particular normals by the supposedly neutral act of measurement.

On the question of emphasis, I heard agreement on the proposition that the contribution of people like us at this meeting lies primarily in improving measurement. Setting norms is difficult; it is not clear who can legitimately set norms.

Third, there was general agreement that there should be more corporate disclosure of socially relevant information. From the point of view of the firm, it's relevant to measure and assess both the firm's impact on society and also the impact that societal constraints have on the firm. The same information is useful to society. Corporate reporting will serve both the corporation and society.

In discussing the corporate disclosure of social information, several problems were noted. First, the corporation is perhaps the logical source for information about its interactions with society but, to be believable, reported information must be validated. In their traditional role of attestors, CPAs have a service to provide by auditing social information. Second, methods and standards of measurement and reporting need development. Corporations are beginning to report social information, but in a variety of ways and with a variety of major assumptions. Corporations will not be able to solve this problem alone. The view was strongly expressed that accountants can be of special help in this area, but that other disciplines must contribute too.

My next major point concerns the macro level of social measurement, social indicators of the quality of life and society. I have listed four sub-points. First, it's apt to be a long time before we have a general measure of the quality of life. We ought not to delude ourselves that it's going to come quickly. Second, we should consider emphasizing the descriptive nature of social indicators. We should perhaps view their primary use to be in finding social problems to explore and to solve rather than as evaluating the state of our society. Third, I heard the proposition that perhaps corporations might have something to contribute to macro social measurement; but, by and large, the contribution is dubious. Macro level measurement in our society should probably not be done by the micro firm. Fourth, I detected a strong agreement that, in macro social measurement, the best thing we can do now is to begin. We can't wait until we have theories perfected. Feedback from measuring now will improve future measurement.

A last major point concerned future progress. I think everyone agrees that we should learn more about what is now going on. There are approximately 1,400 organizations now working with social measurement. Our need for finding out the current state of the art is important.

I also heard several comments concerning the nature of future progress. It was pointed out that, in moving ahead, there will be much resistance to social measurement: reasons why it can't be done, why it can't be done perfectly. Yet, we must move ahead. I heard the view that government should provide the main thrust of moving ahead. I heard divergent views about the way to move ahead. Some would emphasize interdisciplinary efforts. Some point out that a good many people and disciplines are now involved in social measurement efforts—with a fair amount of resulting chaos. I personally suspect both disciplinary and interdisciplinary efforts are needed.

This completes one man's perceptions of the main thrust of the conversations of the past two days. In ending, I'll note one personal reaction. While I seldom heard complete agreement in any area that we discussed, I believe that I and the group are wiser for the frequent divergence of views.

CHURCHILL: Thank you, Justin. It might be useful, taking the summary and our recollections of the past day and a half, to address ourselves, during the short time before adjourning, to discussion of possible next steps. A number of groups are represented here. Is there anything that can be done, and should be done next, with the resources represented here?

EISNER: Neil, I'd like to return to a thought I expressed during our group meeting yesterday, and I hope I don't bore those who heard it then. I suggest efforts to devise a framework for taking account of social services plus the accumulation of capital, everywhere in the economy. The business sector, in its accounting, goes a considerable way toward getting a picture of current production. But this accounting is seriously defective in not capturing, in any systematic way, the accumulation of capital, the investment and resources that will permit more production in the future. By using only arbitrary rules relating to depreciation of physical capital, it fails to account for the changing value of capital. There is no accounting for the accumulation of knowledge within a firm, the effects of research and development, the effects of learning and training on the job.

Now these deficiencies are mild when compared with the deficiencies in accounting for production as a contribution to consumption or capital accumulation in government sectors or in households. What we should do, I think, is to find a measure for the total amount of production in the household that can go to consumption. We are well aware of the vast amount we don't count in the way of household services; there's a great amount of capital accumulation in the household in the way of care of children, the education of the young.

There's a great deal of government production that is not counted and not classified. All that is accounted for is government purchases of goods and services. We don't measure it adequately, and we make no allowance for the production that should be accounted for coming from depreciation of existing government capital or from some imputed rate of return on government capital.

A framework that aggregated all consumption and all accumulation of capital would give us a handle on what to look for—on what Bernie was talking about within The Bank of America, for example, and in our individual units.

In every cost-benefit analysis, we are asking: what does that contribute to current consumption, to current utility, if you wish, and what is contributing to the capital that will enable us to enjoy consumption in the future? Now in many cases these factors are very difficult to quantify. And perhaps you say: why don't the economists try it—try something like measuring the value of investments in trying to cure cancer, or reducing absenteeism, or one thing or another? These are bold efforts, maybe wild, but they would give us a handle on some kind of broad economic or socio-economic indicator. Essentially, my thought is that, if we draw a framework, we will have a notion of what to look for, a tool for evaluating the operations of a nonprofit enterprise, a business enterprise, government programs, the household.

TUNSTALL: As far as what we might do next, my thoughts run, as I indicated yesterday, toward the following framework of work to be done. However, I don't hold any particular doctrine about the patterns of responsibility that this framework suggests. For example, we may assume there are three levels of activity: social reporting, social analysis, and social decision-making. Sometimes these overlap, but it's my view that "social reporting" pertains to conditions in a corporation or a university or a government organization—any institution—and this reporting includes an appraisal of what the members believe they have accomplished. One can report on working conditions of employees (salaries, equal opportunities, etc.), the production process (does it create pollution? etc.), and the product (its uses and its secondary effects on society). "Social analysis," however, might be carried out by an institute or a university in which social scientists analyze social conditions, interpret cause-and-effect relationships, and attempt to spell out plans for change. Thus "analysis" may or may not be carried out by every institution. Universities have been notoriously weak at analyzing their ability to educate and their impact on society. We finally get to the level of "decision-making," and obviously decisions to change a social condition may be made by institutions other than those reporting and analyzing change.

One of the things we discovered as we developed a framework for national social indicators was that the responsibility for social reporting is truly different from the responsibility to analyze, interpret, and decide. I believe there is strong rationale for the federal government to report about the condition of society, on a national basis, but I don't think analysis should be carried out by the federal government for all conditions reported, nor do I believe the power of the federal government need be applied to making all social decisions. I want to make this distinction because it does have a bearing on the role corporations choose to play in the social development field.

WILSON: With respect to next steps, I think disclosure is a key. The tendency of corporations is to keep any information they have close to their chests, and I wonder if this group here oughtn't to venture into the matter of establishing guidelines for corporate disclosure in the social area.

MARLIN: I concur with that proposal, in principle, but surely the guidelines for what social information to disclose and how to present it should not come from CPAs alone. Interdisciplinary communication should continue.

CAMPBELL: I would mention the problem of the gap—the chasm, really—that exists between the accumulation of social data and its communication. It seems to be profoundly difficult for the people who make decisions, whether in the government or a firm, to find out where they should go to get data relevant to the decision that's to be made. Social scientists are frequently criticized—and I think properly—for taking a cavalier attitude toward communicating what they know. Often they are primarily concerned with pushing on from what they now know to something more, and they don't want to be bothered with communicating what they already have. Or, I think, some of them are simply not gifted in communication except with people who have the same degrees and knowledge that they have. And I think that federal agencies are more and more realizing that a good deal of their investment in research, especially in social research, never comes back as information. The increasing pressure from granting agencies—even the National Science Foundation which presumably is interested in primarily basic research—is demonstrating that what the social sciences are doing has relevance to decision-making and should be communicated in such a way that it can be put to use.

TOAN: That's a large issue. It seems to me a man like Dan Tunstall, for example, would write not only for the sociology journals but for the business magazines—describing how data on social objectives and social costs are used in a particular company or institution.

BAUER: The companies and other institutions would have to furnish information. Perhaps a few firms would open up and establish some sort of consortium with university people who would work with them in trying to conceptualize the general problem.

TOAN: I have a couple of additional suggestions for "next steps" for us accountants. One is that the American Institute of CPAs should do more to educate its own members about this whole area. It might be useful, for example, to prepare a bibliography—not one that would get the CPA beyond his depth, but that would constitute an understandable introduction to the processes of social measurement while, at the same time, indicating that the depths do get deeper. Also, as has been suggested, those of us accountants who have become newly acquainted with another's discipline should try to work more with that individual or discipline when it is advantageous to do so. Another project from which we could all benefit would be a "dictionary" of a standard terminology, so that we would avoid failing to communicate because we were using different words for the same thing or the same words to mean different things.

WILSON: I'd like to make one modest, very obvious suggestion, and that is that this network not break up at the end of this meeting. I appreciate that some of you are more closely related to one another than I, for example, am with most of you. To me, one of the great values of this meeting has been just the establishing of these contacts. I do hope we can have agreement to keep each other informed of what we are doing. I guess many of you now are aware that I am pushing for projects of measurement and evaluation within General Electric. I am thinking of efforts of a joint nature, not just within the company. I promise that I will keep you all informed of such progress as we make. I think that future exchanges of information will have real value.

BAUER: My strongest feeling about the meeting is that an excellent job was done in getting together a mix of people whose talents and resources complement one another's. There are at least five people around the table whom I have not met before and with whom I intend to maintain at least some contact. As to how to implement Ian's suggestion for maintaining the network, I don't think we should swear to meet once a year, but I do agree that maintenance of the relationships should be attempted. It will be maintained, I'm sure, on a person-to-person basis, by individual initiative. If there is any device beyond that, I think we should look for it.

*Following additional complimentary remarks about the meeting by several participants, Professor Churchill thanked all for their attendance and participation, and declared the Roundtable ended.*